DEATH AT THE LIGHTHOUSE:

A Grand Island Riddle

Loren Graham

Arbutus Press ~ Traverse City, MI

Death at the Lighthouse: A Grand Island Riddle© 2013, Loren Graham
ISBN 978-1-933926-52-0

Arbutus Press
Traverse City, Michigan
info@arbutuspress.com
www.Arbutuspress.com

Library of Congress Cataloging-in-publication-data

Graham, Loren R.
  Death at the lighthouse : a Grand Island riddle / Loren Graham.
    pages cm
  Includes bibliographical references and index.
  ISBN 978-1-933926-52-0
  1. Murder--Michigan--Grand Island. 2. Lighthouses--Michigan--Grand
Island. I. Title.
  HV6533.M5G73 2013
  364.152'309774932--dc23
                            2013023265

Printed in the United States of America

To the people of the Upper Peninsula — variegated, unruly, proud

Loren Graham is the author of numerous books.
These are the books he has written about
Michigan's Upper Peninsula

A Face in the Rock: The Tale of a Grand Island Chippewa

Grand Island and its Families, 1883-2007
(with Katherine Geffine Carlson)

Contents

INTRODUCTION

I felt I was in the loneliest place in the world, and I was apprehensive. Nothing could be heard except the occasional crash of an unknown creature in the forest, and, once in awhile, a deep thrumming similar to the lowest barely audible sound of a string bass. I was standing alone in 1972 in a semi-ruined lighthouse that my wife, fifteen-year-old daughter, and I had just purchased. The lighthouse was located atop a 200-foot cliff on an island a dozen miles from the Lake Superior shoreline. I was separated from the nearest human being by an unknown but surely great distance, and had hiked several hours through the forest to reach the place, following the path of an old road that once led to the lighthouse but was now no longer passable with a vehicle. The low rumble I occasionally heard, straddling the lowest limit of my auditory range, was caused by an occasional large wave entering a cavern below the lighthouse and resonating in the stony echo chamber.

I wandered around and through the structure. Outside, the grounds had been entirely taken over by waist-high weeds, including thistle plants that stabbed at me as I made my way through the brush. Seen from the exterior, the yellow brick walls were basically intact, although the bricks were cracked and falling out in several places. The window shutters were ripped off revealing that not a pane of glass remained anywhere. The eyeless windows stared vacantly at me. I looked through the open back door and saw that a bear had deposited its scat in the middle of the kitchen floor, which was partially collapsing into the cistern below. Plaster was peeling from the walls, leaving visible large sections of wood lathing fastened with nineteenth-century square nails. On places where the plaster still remained an occasional hiker or hunter who managed to reach the place had left graffiti, several of them dated thirty years earlier. Upstairs the ceiling of one bedroom had totally caved in. Ascending the spiral cast-iron staircase in the brick tower attached to the building I made my way to the top, the old lantern room from which a flame inside a beautiful beehive-shaped Fresnel lens, manufactured in Paris, had once cast its beam out over the lake, visible for twenty miles. Souvenir hunters had long ago taken the lens and stripped the place of its brass fittings, once polished every day by the keeper or his assistant. Standing in the lantern room I looked out at the lake through shattered heavy glass and could see, to the east and to the west, about sixty miles of Lake Superior shoreline, but no structures and no sign of civilization. The view was the same as it had been centuries ago, when only native Chippewa (Ojibway) witnessed it. In the distance I saw the colored cliffs of what had recently become the Pictured Rocks National Lakeshore, a part of the national park system.

The U.S. government built this lighthouse on Grand Island in the Upper Peninsula of Michigan in 1867, replacing one built in 1855, and spared no expense, but the inconvenience of living here both then and now was manifest. In order to bring by ship to the wilderness site the foundation stones, bricks, timber, and ironwork the lighthouse engineers built a special tramway up the cliff, but when the construction work was finished the tramway was removed. The lighthouse then stood alone on its perch far above the lake, cut off from its umbilical cord, and for decades accessible only by foot or horseback through the virgin forests along an eleven mile trail from the south end of the island, which itself was reachable only by boat. A boat could not be brought directly to the light because of the sheer cliff below it.

When we purchased the lighthouse the U.S. Coast Guard still classified it as an operating light but now the light was atop a steel pole some distance from the old lighthouse, considered superfluous to the government's needs. The new light operated automatically but with the same pattern as before: one second on, six seconds off, the "signature" unique to the light that allowed any vessel to identify it. Once a year the Coast Guard serviced its batteries, sometimes coming in by helicopter.

I descended from the tower into the old living room of the lighthouse, totally bare of furniture, and with a wooden wall casement on the north side painted a drab government gray, now scabrous. I then went down four or five more steps into the kitchen. Here the old large black wood-burning kitchen stove still stood, although falling apart. Some of the stove lids were missing and inside I saw several crushed beer cans left by hunters who, for sport, had fired at the stove, leaving holes in the oven door. The only furniture in the kitchen other than the stove was one simple wooden table, covered by an aged checked red-and-white oil cloth that was tacked to the surface. It was stained and unattractive, so I grabbed the edge and ripped it off. To my surprise, under the oil cloth was a large brown envelope, also soiled. Opening it up I found a yellowing newspaper clipping from *The Detroit Free Press* of June 15, 1908. The article headline was as follows:

SLAIN AND SET AFLOAT

Grand Island Lighthouse keeper
And His Assistant are Believed
to be Victims of Brutal Murder
and Robbery

MUTILATED BODY OF ONE FOUND IN BOAT

Keeper George Genery Missing
From His Isolated Post and
Thought to Have Met Same Fate

The clipping was the first indication to me that the deserted tower and house had been the scene of a past violent event still unexplained and awaiting further investigation. Through my wife's family I had long connections to Grand Island. Her grandfather first came to the island in 1883 as a Baptist minister who became a friend of several of the local Chippewa and served intermittently as a preacher for them, baptizing, marrying, and burying them as requested. He met the lighthouse keepers, often Chippewa themselves. Members of my wife's family had been coming back every summer since, and they had a primitive cottage on the southern end of the island. When I arrived in the nineteen fifties I became entranced with the place, but sometimes tripped over the numerous relatives who inhabited the cottage. I wanted to be a writer and I needed privacy. I learned of the existence of a remote lighthouse on the north end of the island which seemed ideal as a place to work and I tried for many years to purchase it. Finally, in 1972, I succeeded.

It was several weeks before I found the courage to spend a night in the abandoned and forlorn structure. In the United States it is difficult to be in a spot where not a sound made by human beings can be heard – no motors, no voices, no background hum. At the lighthouse this silence was the rule. During the day such isolation was often pleasant, but in the evening the envelope of darkness that descended on the place seemed ominous, bringing a sense of unease heightened by my knowledge, incomplete but already present, that something awful and mysterious had already happened in the place. Would I be visited by whatever malevolent forces overwhelmed the keeper and assistant keeper in 1908? On the first night I stayed in the lighthouse alone I slept in a sleeping bag on the floor of the central hallway, the only place where I could close doors in all directions and where there were no windows. I was not sure what I was protecting myself against, but in the first weeks creating such a secure refuge seemed necessary.

The subsequent restoration of the lighthouse and the uncovering of its history were two strands in an intimately intertwined process. Working on one strand would not have been as absorbing as it was without, at the same time, working on the other strand. The physical labor of restoration was deeply involved with the intellectual labor of talking to people who knew parts of the history and studying in archives to find other parts.

What happened in 1908? I began interviewing people, reading old newspapers, and working in archives in Washington, DC; Cleveland, Ohio; Cambridge, Massachusetts; Marquette, Michigan; and in local Michigan historical societies. The two most powerful men in the Upper Peninsula in 1908, when the keepers at North Light disappeared, were William Gwinn Mather and Alexander Agassiz, socially-ambitious Eastern industrialists who lived only a few weeks each year in Michigan. Mather visited with and fell into conflict with George Genry (aka Genery), the keeper of Old North Light.

As I worked I acquired a deeper and deeper appreciation of the local culture of the central Upper Peninsula of Michigan, especially that around Munising, the home of George Genry. This town, it turned out, had been the most productive site for the work of a person often called "the Father of American Folklore," Richard Dorson, and some of the stories he collected came from people connected with the disappearance of Genry.

Gradually a complex and contradictory story emerged that embraced the entire history of the Upper Peninsula of Michigan with its conflicts and problems, and served like a Rorschach pattern differently interpreted by Native Americans, local whites, the U.S. Lighthouse Service, redneck loggers, a patrician strongman, wildlife poachers, excitable newspapers, and an old lady digging for nickels at the base of the lighthouse.

As I puzzled over the details I realized more and more that what was emerging was not a single story, but several ones, each reflecting the view of a different social or ethnic group. The various explanations of what happened to the keeper and assistant keeper of Old North Light in 1908 reflected the strivings and prejudices of the different segments of the local population.

I also realized that what I was describing fits into a broad interpretation of American history at the end of the nineteenth and beginning of the twentieth centuries. The United States at this time was made up of a multitude of inwardly-directed communities that were slowly and painfully being woven together. America was changing from a collection of simple locally-oriented communities guided by regional values into a complex, interdependent society seemingly controlled by distant and impersonal forces.[1]

My telling of this story, then, will be consistent with these two interpretative principles: what a person believes happened at a given moment is often influenced by that person's position in society (a theory of "multiple visions"), and the view that the United States at the end of the nineteenth and beginning of the twentieth centuries was in the process of uniting local communities into a single nation. The Upper Peninsula of Michigan had a mixed ethnic population, including a strong Native American community,

---

[1]   Robert H. Wiebe, *The Search for Order, 1877-1920*, Hill and Wang, New York, 1967.

and it was a place where local unruly values were coming into conflict with forces from the outside trying to impose order. These conflicts and differing visions would fundamentally affect the various explanations people gave, and still give, of the disappearance of the keeper and assistant keeper of the lighthouse on Grand Island.

Loren Graham
Old North Lighthouse
Grand Island, Lake Superior
May, 2013

.

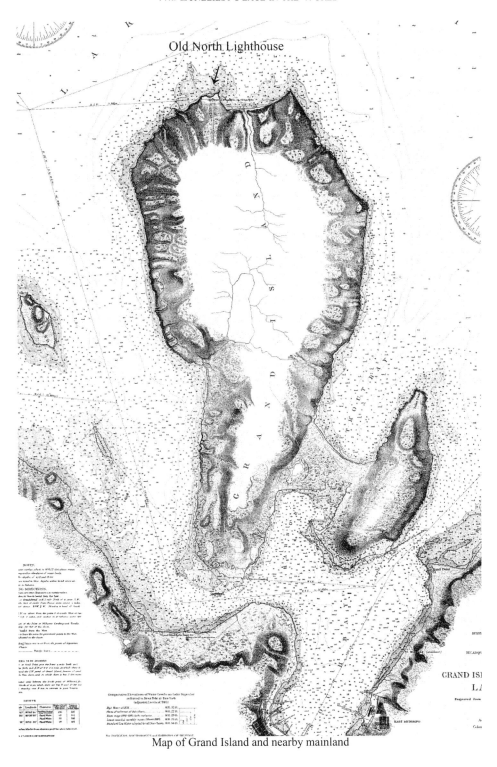

Old North Lighthouse

Map of Grand Island and nearby mainland

Captain Benjamin Trudell of Grand Marais Life Saving Station, who maintained that he had premonitions of all disasters, and who said that dead people communicated with him. He brought Morrison's body back to his station on June 12, 1908.

CHAPTER I:

SLAIN AND SET AFLOAT?

O n June 12, 1908, a wooden sail boat, a small yawl, slowly drifted toward the south shore of Lake Superior about 20 miles north-east of the town of Munising, in the Upper Peninsula of Michigan. The mainmast of the boat was broken and a canvas sail hung loosely over the gunwale. The foremast of the yawl was gone and the boat was half-filled with water, which, as the boat heavily rolled in the waves, sloshed in and out through a small hole in the hull. The boat carried the markings of the U.S. Lighthouse Service. From a distance, which is how the boat was first seen, it appeared that the vessel had been abandoned by its former occupants. Inside the boat and under the seats, however, was the body of a man lying on his face in the water. He was wearing a black satin shirt, blue pants, and fleece-lined underwear. One of his shoes had no lace but instead a length of fish twine.

The beach toward which the boat drifted was a particularly remote location, not near any roads or settlements. Nonetheless, two local hunters, William Van Dusen and Richard Wigman, were walking along the beach and saw the boat. They waded out to the yawl, peered inside at the body, and then pulled the wreck ashore. Together they managed to tilt the vessel enough to drain much of the water and then lifted up the man's head to see if they knew him. Concluding that they did not, they left the body and boat on the beach and notified the closest authority, the keeper of Au Sable Lighthouse, Thomas Irvine, who passed on the news to the Grand Marais Life Saving Station. The head of that station, Captain Benjamin Truedell (aka Trudell) went out to investigate.

Truedell was familiar with the boats of the area, especially U.S. government boats, and upon seeing the stranded vessel was fairly certain it was from the Old North Lighthouse on the northern tip of Grand Island, about 25 miles away to the northwest. Truedell also knew the long-time keeper of that lighthouse, George Genry (aka Genery), and had sometimes worried about his safety since he was aware that even though Genry could not swim he often went out alone in boats. Thinking he would see the face of Genry, he lifted up the man's head and peered at it. The face had turned black and was battered, but Truedell immediately saw that it was not Genry. He did not know who the dead person was. Truedell searched the pockets of the corpse and found only a white handkerchief. He noted that the man was bruised about the head and neck and that his right arm was broken. Also in the boat were an oilcloth coat and a small ax. Truedell noted all this in the official report that he filed after he returned to his station, including the facts that the boat had a hole in the hull four inches long and that the foremast was gone and the mainmast broken. He added that the victim "showes (sic) signs of distress."

Capt. Trudell and Crew in English Life Boat, Grand Marais, Mich.

Captain Trudell and his crew who retrieved Morrison's body on June 12, 1908. Reproduced with permission of Superior View Studios

Truedell notified the Alger County Sheriff, and then ordered his crew of men to take a station life-boat to the site and bring the yawl with the body in it back to the station. Upon the arrival of the boat in Grand Marais (about forty miles from the county seat of Munising) the local coroner, James C. Anderson, immediately impaneled a jury of six men (William Davidson, Charles Shreve, Charles Bork, William Morrisey, James Kems, and O. B. Young) to investigate the circumstances of the unknown person's death.

The jury examined the body and found upon the right arm near the shoulder tattoos of a bird, the American flag and the Union Jack. On the left arm were tattoos of another bird, a full rigged sailing ship, and the letters "U.S.N." The jury heard Truedell, Wigman, and Van Dusen as witnesses but the members obviously did not debate the case long because on the same day they were impaneled, June 13, they gave their verdict. Charles Shreve, secretary of the jury, reported that the man died of "exposure" and "injuries unknown to all here." The verdict was thus unclear about the origins of the "injuries" and what role they may have played in the man's death. The jury concluded its work without learning who the man was.

On the same day that the Grand Marais jury gave its verdict the keeper of the nearby Au Sable Light Station, Thomas E. Irvine, wrote a letter on his role in the incident to his superior, Commander James T. Smith, Inspector of the 11th District of the U.S. Light House Establishment, based in Detroit. Irvine reported that after hearing of the stranded boat from the local hunter William Van Dusen he notified the life savers at Grand Marais and then accompanied Captain Truedell to the site. Keeper Irvine continued that he was "sure that the boat is from Grand Island Light Station and the body evidently the assistant from there." Irvine knew Genry well, and was certain the body was not his, but guessed that the body was that of his assistant, whom he had not met and whose name he did not know.

The report of the condition of the boat that Keeper Irvine gave differed somewhat from that of Captain Truedell. Irvine observed that "the boat is in fair shape, only 1 small hole, the foremast is gone; the mainmast is still standing." Furthermore, Irvine stated that there was sailcloth in the boat that could have been used on the mainmast, but was not. Captain

17

Truedell had reported that the boat was "partly wrecked," the mainmast "unstepped and broke." These differences would later be important in the discussions of whether the occupant might have been able to control the boat if he had not been injured.

On June 18 the Light House Board in Washington, D.C., the institution in charge of all US lighthouses, received the Grand Marais coroner's jury report and also a letter about recent events at North Light from Timothy Dee, keeper of another lighthouse on Grand Island, that of the East Channel (South Light). Dee knew both the keeper and assistant keeper of North Light, and was a close friend and hunting partner of his fellow keeper, George Genry.

Dee reported that on June 13 at 11:30 pm he received word from local fishermen that the beacon at North Light was dark, and that something was wrong there. Furthermore, Dee had heard that same day that a boat from North Light had washed ashore near Grand Marais with a dead man in it. Dee continued in his report to the Light House Board that on June 14 the deputy sheriff of Alger County and several other men had hiked up to North Light to investigate and found that "both keepers were gone." Dee then left for North Light accompanied by George Prior, keeper of the new Munising range light and also an acquaintance of George Genry.

Dee continued that on arriving at North Light he found everything in order "but the lens showed indication of not being used in several days." The last entry in the lighthouse journal was June 3, made by Genry, and the last entry on the log slate was June 5, made by assistant keeper E. S. Morrison. Dee continued that

> Indications show that the asst keeper was in the work shop, and on seeing Mr. Gennery (sic) coming took a wheelbarrow and went to the boathouse. And that neither one ever returned to the light, as the groceries that Mr. Gennery brought from town on June 6th and also the coat he wore that day were found in the Boat House. The station was put in operation and left in charge of Mr. Prior, Mr. MacKenzie and Mr. Prato.

In the boathouse where the groceries were found a box of crackers lay open. The boathouse was located on North Beach, about a half mile from the lighthouse itself; it was the nearest spot to the lighthouse that a boat could be landed.

This poor-quality photograph is the only known one in existence of the Old North Light boathouse, where Genry's and Morrison's coats were found hanging on hooks on June 14, 1908. The boathouse was located on the closest beach to the lighthouse, about a half-mile away. The structure no longer exists. Courtesy of the Alger County Historical Society

Newspapers ran away with the story, describing it in extravagant terms. The *Detroit Free Press* editorialized on June 15, "When has melodrama presented a stranger, more startling story than this story of real life and death, pieced out by investigators from the known facts surrounding a sorrowful discovery? It has the elements of a mystery in motive and deed of violence."

On June 14 the *New York Times* reported, "George Genery (sic), keeper of the North Light on Grand Island, is missing, and his assistant, whose name cannot be learned, is dead, his head beaten to a pulp."

The reporter who wrote the story in the *New York Times* had no idea that an understanding of what happened to George Genry and Edward Morrison could not be fathomed without seeing their fates in the context of time and geography, a context made up of a rowdy frontier culture, conflicts among Native Americans, old generation white settlers and new European immigrants, all disrupted by the intrusion of a New England aristocrat whose mining company was transforming the Upper Peninsula of Michigan. Each of these actors would see the Rorschach pattern differently.

Michigan's Upper Peninsula

CHAPTER II

THE ORPHAN PENINSULA

The Upper Peninsula of Michigan is one of the least known areas of the United States, especially to people living on the east and west coasts, who tend to equate Michigan with Detroit and the rust belt of American industry. Often maps of Michigan are drawn by such people in which the UP (as it is colloquially known) is omitted entirely.

It is an area as different from Detroit as Maine is, and, like Maine, is dominated by forests and a logging culture. Although the UP contains almost one-third of the land mass of the state of Michigan it has only 3% of its population today, with a total of about 308,000 people. Its area is almost half that of Maine, while its population density is less than half of that state. During much of its history the UP has been wilderness, and even yet there are large roadless tracts and a number of officially designated wilderness areas. Moose, mountain lions and wolves can still be found there. Bear and deer are plentiful. Over one-third of the UP today is governmentally-owned forest land, nature preserves, and parks, and much of the rest is held by large timber companies. Grand Island Township, where many events described in this book took place, has a population today of 45, giving it a population density less than that of Alaska. The largest city in the UP is Marquette, with a population of 21,355 in the 2010 census. If the UP became a state, a status which some of its partisans have seriously attempted to promote, it would rank among the fifty other states 42nd in area and 44th in population density. No other large area in the United States east of the Mississippi River is as sparsely populated. At the beginning of the twentieth century, when most of the events in this book occurred, the population of the Upper Peninsula was about 260,000. Its coast line of 1,700 miles contained long stretches without human habitation.

At the time that white men arrived in the Upper Peninsula area, in the seventeenth century, the inhabitants of the area were the Anishinaabeg (Ojibway/Chippewa[1]) who had been there for at least five hundred years. They were a part of a much larger group, today the Chippewa Nation, that extended across the upper middle west and is at present the second largest ethnic group of Indians in the United States. Large numbers are also in Canada, and the presentday border between the two countries meant nothing to them before the arrival of the outsiders and subsequent geo-political division.

The Chippewa in the area were hunter-gatherers who fished in the lakes and rivers in the summer, hunted inland in the winters, and gathered maple sugar in the spring, Family and tribal affiliations were strong, resulting in developed cultural traditions. Social organization was grounded in the clan or "totemic" system according to which each Chippewa was a member of a group named after a totem animal – such as bear, wolf, martin, crane, and eagle. Marriage within a clan was strictly forbidden. Although the Chippewa did not have a written language they were moving toward one based on pictographs that were used both in birch-bark "documents" and stone inscriptions, some of which can still be found along the shores of Lake Superior. A few of their many songs and legends have been recorded by anthropologists.

The traditional enemies of the Chippewa were the Sioux to the west and the Iroquois to the east. These conflicts predated the arrival of the white men, but were greatly exacerbated by the pressure of white settlement coming from the east and pushing the Iroquois westward. In turn, the Chippewa moved westward, and conflicts with the Sioux were frequent.

---

1   Since the Native Americans of the region did not have a written language, much disagreement exists concerning how terms and names should be written in English. The terms "Ojibway" and "Chippewa" are different ways of spelling the same word, the first thought to have been taken from the French, the second from the English. The Catholic priest Frederic Baraga, who published a dictionary of the native language in the late nineteenth century, often used the term "Otchipwe." The word "Anishinaabeg" is usually translated as "First" or "Original-Peoples." In this book I often use the term "Chippewa" because the official name today of the local tribe of the area, headquartered in Sault Ste. Marie, is "The Sault Tribe of Chippewa Indians."

The earliest recorded arrival of white men was in 1622 when Etienne Brule came to the eastern end of the peninsula, where now is the town of Sault Ste. Marie, Michigan. For many years, until the late eighteenth century, the links between the Chippewa and the French were strong and, on the whole, the relationship was good.[2] The French traded guns, knives, liquor, cloth and cooking utensils with the Chippewa and received furs in return. The impact of the French traders on the area was enormous, and even today their influence is manifest in the dozens of French place names to be found in the Upper Peninsula and in the large number of French family surnames among the residents. The French readily intermarried with the Chippewa and often learned the native language. Many of the early prominent figures in Upper Peninsula history were of "mixed blood" and were commonly called "Métis people."

The relationship between the Chippewa and the British, who prevailed over the French in the Treaty of Paris of 1763, was much more problematic. The British tended to treat the Chippewa in a colonial manner. Despite occasional clashes, some of them bloody, actual warfare was usually avoided, and this uneasy but restrained relationship was maintained with the Americans as well.

Michigan's possession of much of the Upper Peninsula is an accident of a bizarre conflict, "The Toledo War" of 1835. Before Michigan's admission to the union in 1837 the Upper Peninsula was part of the Wisconsin Territory, to which it was geographically attached. Had the Toledo War not happened the Upper Peninsula would today surely be part of Wisconsin, not Michigan. Michigan Territory and the Upper Peninsula were separated by water, a separation that even yet has impact. In a bitter border dispute the populous and powerful state of Ohio ripped off a strip of Michigan territory along the Michigan-Ohio border, an area where the city of Toledo is now located. Ohio was already in the union and possessed political clout which the Michigan Territory lacked. As one politician observed, "All parties are courting the electoral votes of Ohio, Indiana and Illinois and poor Michigan must be sacrificed."[3]

---

2   *Relations des jésuites: contenant ce qui s'est passé de plus remarquables dans les missions des pères de la Compagnie de Jésus dans la Nouvelle-France*, A. Côté, Quebec, 1858.
3   Lucius Lyon, quoted in Don Faber in the source in the next footnote, p. 139.

Both the state of Ohio and the territory of Michigan mustered hundreds of men for the developing fight, many of whom were totally lacking in training and even in arms. Those without guns carried pitch forks and scythes. The scruffy bands maneuvered around each other, and nearly had a violent confrontation at "The Battle of Phillips Corners" on April 26, 1835. Passions ran high but bravery was short. Whenever either side fired a shot or two the other side usually turned and ran. The two sides loved to fire hundreds of shots at each other when they were safely out of range. In the entire "war" there was only one actual casualty: the knifing of a Michigan deputy sheriff by an inebriated Ohioan. The deputy sheriff survived. The Ohioan, a colorful man named Two Stickney, was protected by Ohio authorities from the wrath of the Michiganders, who put a price on his head.[4]

The war was the subject of doggerel attributed to George B. Catlin:

And who would cut up Michigan
"I," says Governor Lucas
"What I undertook is
To cut up little Michigan."

And who has bid him do it?
A million freemen,
(Counting women and children)
'Tis Ohio bids him do it.

And who rings the bells of war?
"I," says General Bell
"Tis I that rings the bell,
Ding, dong goes my bell of war."

---

4   The details of the dispute, and the doggerel below, are documented in: Don Faber, *The Toledo War: The First Michigan-Ohio Rivalry,* The University of Michigan Press, Ann Arbor, 2008.

The unequal battle was easily won by Ohio, and, as a result, Michigan lost a strip of land, varying from five to eight miles in width, stretching from the Indiana border to Lake Erie, and giving Ohio a new port on Lake Erie. Recognizing that Michigan had been done an injustice, and noting that Wisconsin was also a territory, not a state, and one with even less power than Michigan Territory, the U.S. Congress committed yet another territorial ripoff by awarding, in compensation, almost all of the Upper Peninsula to the new state of Michigan. As one later historian wrote, "Both parties acquired lands (Ohio the Toledo Strip, Michigan the Upper Peninsula) that neither had any legal right to."[5] Even though the disparity in size of land of the two disputed parcels was enormous (The Toledo Strip taken from Michigan was 468 square miles, the Upper Peninsula land given to it was almost 9000 square miles) most people believed that Michigan had been cheated. A group of irate Michigan citizens complained to Congress that they had been given "a mess of pottage on the frozen and sterile shores of Lake Superior which is not naturally connected with Michigan and could be of no use to her as part of her State."

In the nearly two centuries since the Toledo War residual territorial disputes in the area have rather frequently revived. In 1844, 1889, 1915, 1922, 1932, 1947, 1965, 1971, and 2003 the issues again came up, in different ways. In the latest flareup, in 2003, a US Congressman maintained that Ohio acted "illegally" in the Toledo War. Thus, the passions evoked by the Toledo War may not even yet be totally dissipated. Some people say that the fierce rivalry between the football teams of Michigan and Ohio State comes partially from the Toledo War.

One vestige of the Toledo War still strangely affects Michigan and Ohio today. When the victorious Ohioans redrew to their benefit the line between Michigan and Ohio they did so rather carelessly, drawing a straight line from Indiana to the edge of Lake Erie. They either did not notice or did not care that out in the lake there was a tiny peninsula pointing northwards from the Ohio mainland; if the line they drew to the edge of the lake were extended, it clipped off the top bit of that peninsula. Thus, these 240 acres of land by default fell to Michigan. Even though clearly within the state

---

5   W. V. Way, quoted in Faber, op. cit., p. 174.

of Ohio, it still exists as Michigan territory today, and is known as the "Lost Peninsula." Practically a part of Toledo, it is not served by any Ohio services, such as Toledo garbage collection. It cannot be reached from the main part of Michigan except by boat or by driving through Ohio. A true relic of the Toledo War, it resists periodic attempts to be incorporated into Toledo and Ohio.

The Upper Peninsula, like the Lost Peninsula, was another orphan awarded to Michigan as a result of the Toledo War of 1835. But who actually owned the Upper Peninsula at that time? It was mostly "Indian Territory," the home of the Chippewa (Ojibway). Somehow their claim to the land needed to be eliminated if the Upper Peninsula was to become a true part of the new state of Michigan, entering the union in 1837. This was largely accomplished in the Ottawa-Chippewa Treaty of Washington of 1836, a sweeping agreement that ceded almost thirteen million acres of land in both the lower and upper peninsulas of Michigan to the United States, including almost all of the Upper Peninsula east of a line between Bay de Noc and Marquette. An article in that treaty of which today most white people are unaware directly bore on Grand Island, its territory, and the hunting and fishing rights of Native Americans there. And these provisions would provide part of the fabric of the central story in this book.

Nineteen years after the treaty was signed, a lighthouse station was established on the island, the same station which my family would end up purchasing. Records of the lighthouse showed that several of the early keepers were of Native American descent or married to Native Americans, including the mysteriously disappeared George Genry, who was part Chippewa. These Chippewa lighthouse keepers knew about the disputes between whites and local natives over the island.

The white men who negotiated the 1836 treaty were Lewis Cass and Henry Schoolcraft, two persons with a longstanding association with the Upper Peninsula and a reputation for extinguishing land claims of the American Indians. Cass served as governor of Michigan Territory from 1813 to 1831 and was U.S. Secretary of War in 1836. Later, in 1848, he was the nominee of the Democratic Party for the U.S. presidency. Schoolcraft was originally a geologist but became an expert on Indian affairs. He participated, together with Cass, in an expedition in 1820 along the southern shore of Lake Superior during which he collected information about the Chippewa of the area, including those on Grand Island, who made a very positive impression upon him. He described one of them as "a tall and beautiful youth" and continued "of all the tribes of Indians whom I have visited, I have never felt, for any individual, such a mingled feeling of interest and admiration."[6]

Cass later appointed Schoolcraft Indian agent in Sault Ste. Marie, a position he held for many years. While in Sault Ste. Marie Schoolcraft married the grand-daughter of a famous Chippewa chief and learned from her the Chippewa language and much about native folklore. Eventually he published a six-volume work on the history of the native tribes of the United States.

Although Schoolcraft professed great appreciation for Indian culture, and admired many Indians individually, in his practical work as Indian agent he fully supported the harsh policies of the American government toward native tribes. During the first half of the nineteenth century those policies were based on the idea that the pagan culture of the Indians was incompatible with Christianity and "civilization," and that therefore the Indians in the eastern half of the United States should be removed from their ancestral homes and sent west. The assumption underlying this policy was that Indians were an inferior race, biologically and culturally. According to President Andrew Jackson in 1835, "All preceding experiments for the improvement of the Indians have failed. It seems now to be an established fact that they cannot live in contact with a civilized community and prosper."

According to the 1836 Treaty of Washington with the exception of several tiny reservations all the lands belonging to the Grand Island, Bay de Noc, Mackinac, and Sault bands of Chippewa passed to the whites. Yet

---

6   This young Grand Island Chippewa told Schoolcraft about the dramatic recent history of his band (which Cass and other members of the party recorded); that story is the subject of another book of mine, *A Face in the Rock*. For Cass's report, see: Mentor L. Williams (ed.), *Narrative Journal of Travels through the Northwestern Regions of the United States Extending from Detroit through the Great Chain of American Lakes to the Sources of the Mississippi River in the Year 1820,* by Henry R. Schoolcraft, Michigan State College Press, East Lansing, 1953, csp. pp. 104-110.

the treaty included a provision that the Chippewa could continue to fish and hunt these lands until they were required for settlement. By the time those settlements were established, much of the suitable land in the western United States had already been claimed by others, so the Chippewa were never forcibly sent west. Hard as their lot was, they were not subjected to removal and to the "Trail of Tears" experienced by the Cherokees and other eastern Native Americans. But they retained only several thousand acres of their land, and within a few decades they were reduced to poverty. Much later they would have a resurgence and today in several counties of the Upper Peninsula they are between ten and fifteen percent of the population.

In negotiating the 1836 treaty Schoolcraft made full use of his kinship ties to the Chippewa. At the same time that he represented the U.S. government, his wife's uncle and other relatives represented the Chippewa bands with which he negotiated. In pursuing the government's goals Schoolcraft thus had enormous advantages. What is more, Schoolcraft and Cass plied the Chippewa chiefs with liquor to soften their resistance, even though both had often spoken against such policies.[7]

In their attitudes Schoolcraft and Cass were typical of white politicians in the first half of the nineteenth century. On the one hand, they expressed sentimental views about the disappearance of the "noble red man" and actually did valuable research in collecting information about Native American culture; on the other, they were convinced that Indian culture was doomed by the advance of "civilization," and energetically and unfeelingly promoted the destruction of that culture. Thus, Schoolcraft and Cass, despite their statements of admiration for Indian culture and Schoolcraft's marriage to a Chippewa, actively promoted what a leading academic historian of Michigan's Indian communities has recently called "perhaps the most morally despicable story in North American history."[8]

---

7   Bernard C. Peters, "Hypocrisy on the Great Lakes Frontier: The Use of Whiskey by the Michigan Department of Indian Affairs," *The Michigan Historical Review,* Vol. 18, No. 2 (Fall, 1992), pp. 1-13.

8   Charles E. Cleland, *Rites of Conquest: The History and Culture of Michigan's Native Americans,* The University of Michigan Press, Ann Arbor, 1992, p. 198.

Reproduced with permission of Marquette County Historical Society

Reproduced with permission of Superior View Studios

By the end of the nineteenth century most of the dispossessed Chippewa were living in unspeakable poverty, as shown in the accompanying pictures.

Grand Island was one of the few places with land reserved for Chippewa, at least for a time, by the Treaty of Washington. Article Three of the treaty stated that such reservations included, "Six hundred and forty acres, on Grand Island, and two thousand acres, on the main land south of it." This grant was later ignored, and was not renewed by the US government, which the Treaty stipulated was an option. Thus, the claim of the Chippewa to Grand Island land eroded over time, but it was a claim that they occasionally raised again. Furthermore, since the treaty granted the Chippewa the right to hunt and fish throughout the entire area until such time as it was needed for settlement, the natives could argue that much of the area was never used for settlement. Thus the Treaty of Washington contained ambiguous phrases that would later be the source of much contention. Some of these phrases would be connected to the fate of George Genry.

Less than ten years after the Toledo War and the Treaty of Washington the Upper Peninsula, regarded by many whites as "of no use," was found to contain exceptional riches. Once again the acquisition of this wealth involved a swindle.

In the summer of 1844 a party of white surveyors sketched out township lines between the mouth of the Escanaba River and the spots where later the cities of Marquette and Negaunee developed. The party was directed by William A. Burt, a surveyor for the state of Michigan with a secure history as a mapper of the area, and seven other people. The members of the party reported that on September 18 they noticed variations in the magnetic needle of their compass and looked for the cause. One member of the party, Harvey Mellen, later a state senator, is reported to be the first to find iron ore.

Abundant evidence exists that these white men did not find this iron ore by themselves but were directed to the spot by a Chippewa named Mah-je-ge-zhik.[9] One of the members of the surveying party, Jacob Houghton, who was only 17 years old at the time, later denied that anybody was with them. In fact, in a letter written 56 years later, Houghton maintained that during the entire summer of 1844 while exploring this area "we saw no human being."[10] Houghton added in 1900 "I am now the sole survivor of the party of 1844."

Houghton was lying when he said they saw no one else. The area around what is now Marquette contained many members of the Chippewa tribe. They often had their villages near the mouths of rivers flowing into Lake Superior and Lake Michigan, such as the presentday Escanaba, Carp, Chocolay, and Little Garlic Rivers. These spots were particularly good for fishing. In the fall and winter the Chippewa often moved inland to hunt deer, and harvested maple sugar in the spring. Perhaps the reason that Houghton said in 1900 that they saw "no human being" in the summer of 1844 was that he did not consider Indians to be humans. It is revealing that when Houghton identified who the members of the surveying party were, he named "Wm. Ives, R. S. Mellen, Harvey Mellen, James King and myself and two packers." The unnamed "two packers" were Chippewa Indians. Most important to Houghton, however, was to deny the rights of the descendants of Mah-je-ge-zhik to a share of the riches that came from the iron ore. Houghton's letter of 1900 in the Western Reserve Historical Society is on the stationery of the Cleveland-Cliffs Iron Company, the company that controlled the iron mines, and whose president, William G. Mather, would in just a few years become angry with the Chippewa keeper of North Light on Grand Island, George Genry.

Very near the spot where the iron ore was located by the surveying party one of the most productive mines in the United States was constructed: the Jackson Mine, first operated by a man named Philo Everett. It was also the fall hunting ground of Mah-je-ge-zhik and his band of Chippewa. And the theory that Mah-je-ge-zhik helped the white men is greatly strengthened

---

9   Often called in English "Marjigesisk." Also: "Man-je-ge-zhik" and "Marji Gezick" and other variations.

10   Letter from Jacob Houghton to M. M. Duncan, July 31, 1900, in collection of Western Reserve Historical Society, Cleveland, Ohio.

by the fact that two years later, in 1846, he was paid with stock in the Jackson Mining Co. "in consideration of services rendered…in hunting ores." Mah-je-ge-zhik kept with him at all times the paper awarding him "twelve undivided one-hundredth part" of the Jackson Mining Company, and showed it to many people. But by the time a descendant of Mah-je-ge-zhik, Charlotte Kawbawgam, tried to sell that stock the Jackson Mining Company had been absorbed by the Cleveland-Cliffs Iron Company (headed by William Gwinn Mather) and the courts determined that the stock was worthless even though Philo Everett defended Kawbawgam's claim.[11] As a result, Native Americans were deprived of financial benefit from the iron industry. Later, a small cash payment was made to some of Mah-je-ge-zhik's descendants. The Cleveland Cliffs Iron Company still exists (since 2008 named "Cliffs Natural Resources"), and in 2012 had a market capitalization of over 8 billion dollars.

Reacting to the discovery of iron ore, U S. business interests decided that the only way to exploit the mineral riches of the Lake Superior region was to construct a deep canal at the Sault rapids on the St. Mary's River connecting Lake Superior and Lake Huron. A group of eastern investors formed a private company, the St. Mary's Falls Ship Canal, to dig a navigable channel between the two lakes, and in June 1853 a crew of four hundred men under the direction of Charles T. Harvey began excavating the ditch. The path of the canal ran right through the traditional village, fishing, and burial grounds of the local Chippewa. Notwithstanding their protests, the canal was rapidly built, and in May 1855 the locks at Sault Ste. Marie were opened. For the first time Lake Superior became accessible to large ships from distant ports. In that same summer, reacting to the pleas of the mining companies, the U.S. government constructed a lighthouse on the north end of Grand Island, which lay directly in the path of ships going between the new canal at Sault Ste. Marie and the new ore port of Marquette. The dangerous cliffs and storms caused the area to be called "the graveyard coast." The newspaper in Marquette, *The Mining Journal,* said on July 29,

---

11   The story is the basis of the novel by Robert Traver, *Laughing Whitefish*, McGraw-Hill, New York, 1965.'

1871, that "…in all navigation of Lake Superior, there is none more dreaded by the mariner than from Whitefish Point to Grand Island."

The bountiful mineral riches of the Upper Peninsula were not confined to iron ore. A little more than a hundred miles northwest of Grand Island was the Keweenaw Peninsula, a prominent and rugged finger of land projecting far out into Lake Superior. It contained the largest deposit of natural copper in the world, so pure that often it could be pounded into implements directly, without refinement. Native Americans had done so for thousands of years, trading their copper products throughout North America.[12]

During the last decades of the nineteenth century the Calumet and Hecla Mining Company in the Keewenaw was the leading copper producer in the United States, and, from 1869 to 1876, the biggest copper company in the world. And, just as was the case for the Cleveland-Cliffs Iron Company, a well-educated Easterner with Harvard connections headed the Calumet and Hecla Mining Company. He was Alexander Agassiz of Cambridge, Massachusetts, son of Louis Agassiz and stepson of Elizabeth Cabot Cary Agassiz. Louis Agassiz was one of the most famous naturalists in America, and his wife Elizabeth Cabot Cary, who became the first president of Radcliffe College, was a member of one of Boston's leading families.

The Agassiz and Cabot families had long-standing interests in Lake Superior. In 1848 Louis Agassiz, a new professor of zoology of Harvard College who had already achieved recognition in his native Switzerland, led an expedition of sixteen men to study the natural history of Lake Superior[13]. Eleven of the sixteen were faculty, students, or recent graduates at Harvard. One of them was J. Elliott Cabot, a Boston Brahmin who would later be an Overseer of Harvard University.

When the Harvard men returned to Cambridge from the Lake Superior expedition they told fascinating tales to their friends and colleagues about the beauties of the area. Among Agassiz's friends listening to these

---

12   David J. Krause, *The Making of a Mining District: Keewenaw Native Copper,* 1500-1870, Wayne State University Press, Detroit, 1992.
13   Louis Agassiz, Lake Superior: *Its Physical Character, Vegetation, and Animals, Compared with Those of Other and Similar Regions*, Gould, Kendall and Lincoln, Boston, 1850.

accounts was Henry Wadsworth Longfellow, whose awakened interests in Lake Superior eventually ended up in his writing of his world-famous poem Hiawatha.

Louis Agassiz was a strong believer in creationism. He wrote that when the naturalist looks at Lake Superior, "He beholds indeed the work of a being thinking like himself, but he feels at the same time that he stands as much below the Supreme Intelligence in wisdom, power and goodness, as the works of art are inferior to works of nature." (Agassiz's creationism became better known after 1859, when he opposed it to the form of evolution presented by Charles Darwin in *On the Origin of Species*.) Agassiz was also a racist, a person who believed that blacks, Indians, and certain other ethnic groups were inferior intellectually and morally to whites.

Louis's son Alexander was born in Switzerland to Louis's first wife, but when she died he came, at the age of 14, to join his father in the United States. He graduated from Harvard in 1859, where he studied engineering and chemistry. He was not the ardent anti-evolutionist that his father was, but, similar to his father, he regarded humans as ethnically differentiated in intelligence and morality. His step-mother Elizabeth Cabot Cary helped him to move easily in the elite social circles of Boston, where he met her friends and relatives Quincy Adams Shaw and E. J. Hulbert, both interested in the copper ore deposits in the Upper Peninsula. A group of Boston men, including Hulbert, Shaw and Alexander Agassiz, formed what later became the Calumet and Hecla Mining Company.

Alexander Agassiz turned out to be a skilled engineer and manager and ended up as president of the company, a position he held from 1871 to his death in 1910. Thus, in 1908, when George Genry disappeared from the lighthouse serving the ships of the iron and copper industries, two Eastern industrialists—William Mather and Alexander Agassiz— were the most influential men in the Upper Peninsula. They employed thousands of workers and controlled almost every aspect of their lives– their employment, housing, medical care, education and even recreational and religious activities.

Alexander Agassiz, like William Mather, prided himself on his care for his workers. The mines were located in wilderness areas without

Statue of Alexander Agassiz in Calumet, Michigan.
Photo by Keith Payne, Interpretive Ranger, Keweenaw National Historical Park..

social amenities, and therefore the mining companies had to create entire towns. They built houses for workers on company land, rented them at low rates, provided for schools, libraries, and churches. They promoted, and sometimes owned, stores selling food and household goods. Agassiz, at least at first, tried to keep his workers' wages above the norm for manual labor in the area. He was an exponent of enlightened paternalism.[14]

14   Larry Lankton, *Hollowed Ground: Copper Mining and Community Building on Lake Superior, 1840s-1990s,* Wayne State University Press, Detroit, 2010; *Cradle to Grave: Life, Work and Death at the Lake Superior Copper Mines,* Oxford University Press, Oxford and New York,1991; Alison K. Hoagland, *Mine Towns: Buildings for Workers in Michigan's Copper Country,* University of Minnesota Press, Minneapolis and London, 2010.

Underground mining was an ugly, demeaning, and dangerous activity. The historian of technology Lewis Mumford wrote: "Mine: blast: dump: crush: extract: exhaust – there was indeed something devilish and sinister about the whole business."[15] Obtaining workers willing to go down hundreds of feet into the dimly lit shafts was not always easy. Native Americans, numerous in the area but accustomed to the green forests, would have nothing to do with mining. Established workers engaged in above-ground employment often also would not become miners. The mining companies had to import hundreds of men from abroad. At first Cornishmen, familiar with the tin and copper mines of Cornwall, were important in the business, sometimes as underground bosses. Later, it was necessary to bring in large numbers of workers from Eastern and Southern Europe, including Finns, Poles, Hungarians, Slovenians and Croatians..

As the years went by Alexander Agassiz's earlier benevolent paternalism toward his workers showed a harsher and harsher face. Even though he was present in Calumet only a few weeks a year, preferring his Cambridge and Newport homes, he micro-managed everything from afar. He read the local Michigan newspapers, encircled articles that agitated him, and demanded explanations from his supervisors at the mines. He feared unions and "radical" viewpoints and personally approved the books that were purchased for his workers' library, carefully blocking any reading material that he considered subversive. When streetcars were proposed for the town of Calumet he strenuously fought against a transportation system that might allow the workers to gather together for meetings, fearing that labor agitation would be the result. He told his managers never to give in to workers' demands since this would show signs of "weakness" inviting further demands. He tried to defuse worker discontent by improving wages and social conditions at moments chosen by him when it did not look like he was making concessions to worker demands.

Agassiz's policies were gradually undermined by changes occurring throughout the nation. The period of his tenure as president of Calumet and

---

15   Lewis Mumford, *Technics and Civilization,* Harcourt, Brace & World, New York, 1963, pp. 74-75.

Hecla, 1871-1910, coincided with the explosion of the American labor union movement. Although Agassiz kept up with technological changes in the mines, he did not stay abreast with social and political events there. He was busy with scientific research back in Cambridge and regarded the mines as a source of funds for his natural history investigations and gifts to Harvard.[16] Agassiz managed to keep unions out of his mines during his lifetime, but the unions which were already strong in other mining areas, such as the Western Federation of Miners, began to sense that Agassiz was engaged in a losing battle. The political sensitivities of the workers were also changing. Earlier miners, such as the Cornishmen and the first generation of Finns, were often loyal, religious, and obedient. A new generation was much more willing to question the policies and motives of their employers. Finland at this time was a part of the Russian empire, and the new arrivals at Calumet and Hecla told stories of their oppression by their former tsarist masters and of the new radical, sometimes Marxist, ideas that were circulating among Finnish workers back home. Agassiz came to fear these new Finns and tried to restrict their numbers in his mines, not an easy task since there were more Finns in the local population than any other ethnic group.

Mining technology was also changing in a way that increased worker discontent. The old method of working at the mine face was entirely manual. Miners used sledges to pound long spikes into the rock in front of them, breaking up the ore, which was then deposited in small cars and removed by "trammers," the lowliest of the workers. The miners at the rock face worked in groups of three or four men, often friends or even relatives. They looked after each other's safety. The greatest danger was a collapse of the rock ceiling directly above them. Experienced miners knew that such rock falls were usually preceded by a cracking noise; therefore, one of the group at work took as his special responsibility listening for these warning signs and keeping an eye on the rock ceiling. But in the last decades of the nineteenth century the spikes and sledges were replaced by pneumatic drills. At first the automatic drills were large and heavy tools requiring several men to operate; later the "one-man pneumatic drill" appeared. The mine superintendents, in

16   G. R. Agassiz (ed.), *Letters and Recollections of Alexander Agassiz with a Sketch of His Life and Work,* Houghton Mifflin Co., Boston and New York, 1913.

the name of efficiency, wanted the miners at the rock face to work alone with these new drills. The miners despised the one-man drills. They lost social interaction with their fellow workers and they feared the rock falls even more than before. The drills made so much noise that the miners could not hear the warning crack that had so often saved them in the past, and

One man pneumatic drill which the miners so hated and which was a cause of the strike. Reproduced with permission of Superior View Studio.

Miners on strike in 1896. Reproduced with permission of Superior View Studio

they had no colleagues with them to help see danger and rescue them if disaster came. What had been merely dangerous before became lonely and dangerous, a fearful combination.

By the first years of the twentieth century the mines were a place of ferment and discontent. Fatal accidents were occurring in the mine shafts at a rate of about one death every week.[17] For every death there were approximately seventy injuries. At a time of rising concerns in the nation about health and well-being (the "progressive era") such casualty rates became increasingly unacceptable. Something had to be done.

Alexander Agassiz died before the pot boiled over. The man who dealt with the situation was "Big Jim" MacNaughton, a hard master appointed by Agassiz to control the workers. MacNaughton's opinion was that "the Union must be killed at all costs."[18] He almost literally succeeded.

Home of copper miner showing bullet holes resulting from labor strike in 1913. Reproduced with permission of Superior View Studio

---

17   See Lankton, *Cradle to Grave*, chapter 7, *"The Cost of Copper: One Man Per Week."*

18   Lankton, *Hollowed Ground*, p. 195.

In 1913 the miners at the Calumet and Hecla Mining Company went out on strike, demanding an eight hour day, a minimum pay of $3 a day, a prohibition of one-man pneumatic drills, and recognition of their union.[19] The strike dragged on for months but the company supervisors refused to yield to the demands. Fights and isolated shootings broke out. The governor of Michigan called out the National Guard to preserve order, and the uniformed men pitched their tents around the mining buildings. Still the workers continued their strike. Increasingly radicalized, the workers became more sympathetic to the Western Federation of Miners, which wanted intensely to get into the Calumet mines. The company organized a conservative counter-organization, the Citizens Alliance, which tried to build anti-strike sentiment, strongest among the above-ground workers, mechanics and supervisors.

On Christmas Eve, 1913, the striking workers organized an afternoon Christmas party for their families. The festivity was held on the second floor of a social club in downtown Calumet. At the height of the holiday celebration a man wearing the pin of the Citizens Alliance shouted "Fire!" There was no fire, but the party-goers panicked and rushed for the stairway down to the street. In the crush 73 of them were suffocated, 62 of them children. Finns were the largest ethnic group among the victims.

A local Finnish newspaper placed the blame directly on the Citizens Alliance and the mine management. Local authorities arrested the entire staff of the newspaper and closed it down.

The Christmas Eve catastrophe shocked the nation. Labor sympathizers from all over the country converged on Calumet and marched in a funeral procession that included 32,000 people, more than the population of the entire town. The event became iconic in the history of the American labor movement and decades later still evoked strong emotions, as evidenced by Woody Guthrie's 1941 song "1913 Massacre." An historian in 2006 called the event "Michigan's Largest Mass Murder."[20]

The deaths of so many of the members of their families broke the spirits of the striking workers. A few holdouts stayed out of the mines for

---

19   The best account of the strike is: Steve Lehto, *Death's Door: The Truth Behind Michigan's Largest Mass Murder,* Momentum Books, Troy, 2006.

20   See Lehto, *Death's Door.*

several more months, but gradually the strike declined and then collapsed. The company had won, the workers had lost.

Although the 1913 massacre occurred after the 1908 disappearance of the lighthouse keepers, it contributed to the atmosphere of distrust between workers and mine owners that had been building for decades. Troopers were called to keep order in the iron mines long before 1908—in 1874, 1894 and 1895. The controversy over what happened to George Genry and Edward Morrison continued long after all those events, including the tragedy of 1913, and was influenced by them.

The Upper Peninsula was a place in which people with conflicting visions—Native Americans, mining and logging entrepreneurs, workers, ethnic groups, and local politicians,—were constructing their own versions of what was important for the future of the area. These visions would be supplemented by yet others and created a situation in which a single event, the disappearance of lighthouse keepers, would result in disputing interpretations.

Miners' children crushed to death in the Christmas Eve Massacre of 1913. Reproduced with permission of Superior View Studio

CHAPTER III

THE CONQUEST OF THE UPPER PENINSULA

he upper peninsula of Michigan boasts at its eastern end several of the oldest European settlements in the United States, Sault Ste. Marie founded in 1668, and St. Ignace, established in 1671. St. Ignace was named after St. Ignatius of Loyola, creator of the Jesuit religious order. The original church there has been moved and rebuilt several times, but it still maintains baptismal records going back to 1695[1]. However, the influence of these villages on the rest of the upper peninsula in the early years of white settlement was limited by the absence of good roads to them from any direction, although they were the centers of much boat traffic. They were cut off by water from the lower peninsula and to the west by vast forests and swamps. Even today St. Ignace has a population of less than three thousand people, almost 20% of them Native Americans.

The real conquest of the Upper Peninsula awaited the advent of railroads in the last half of the nineteenth century. The first railroads came in the eighteen fifties but initially they were just short runs between inland mines and ports such as Marquette and Calumet, and did not do anything for the area as a whole. Then lines began spreading from the west where the peninsula had its land connection with the rest of the country through Wisconsin. In the 1870's and 1880's several companies tried to build west-east roads but it was not until 1887 that one could ride from Sault Ste. Marie to Duluth and not until 1889 that Sault Ste. Marie was linked to Minneapolis and St. Paul.

Marquette and the Keewenaw were the locations of iron and copper mines promoted by money coming from outside investors, often from Cleveland, Chicago, Boston, and New York. These tycoons wanted railroads and large lake ports to get their iron and copper out and supplies in.

---

1   See Ronald Jolly and Karl Bohnak, *Michigan's Upper Peninsula Almanac,* University of Michigan Press, Ann Arbor, 2009.

Several of the mining companies soon developed large timber operations as well, supplying the company smelters with wood and charcoal. The forests of the Upper Peninsula were the sources of lumber for the building of the burgeoning cities and towns of the lower Middle West. Railroads connected logging camps to their markets at a time when there were no other roads.

The railroads became so essential as a means of transportation in an area that was largely trackless wilderness that ordinary citizens, even families, devised their own home-made means to use them to get from place to place without having to purchase tickets, as shown below.

Reproduced with permission of Superior View Studio

The mining and timber companies were led by men who had often been educated in the East and who wanted to demonstrate that although they were moving into the wilderness of the upper peninsula they brought some culture with them. As banks, law firms, and commerce developed in a few small cities the desire of the mining executives, leading bankers, and wealthiest merchants to distinguish themselves from the scruffy, sometimes illiterate men they employed in distant mines and lumber camps was expressed in their financing of opera houses, libraries, mansions, and exclusive hunting and fishing clubs.

In the lumber camps and mines where the top officials went only rarely, an environment prevailed that was dominated by hard manual labor during the day and liquor, fisticuffs, and whoring in any free time. It was sometimes said that when one took the train from Marquette eastward, through the towns of Au Train, Munising, Wetmore, Shingleton, and Seney, the farther one got from Marquette the rougher the scene became.

Logs being taken out near Munising at the end of the nineteenth century. Reproduced with permission of Superior View Studio

Perhaps the most notorious of all was Seney. As one of its local historians boasted, Seney "out-cut, out-logged, out-fought, and out-whored" the rest of the world in its heyday, which was the eighteen eighties and nineties. At one time it had twenty-one saloons and five brothels. It prided itself on having no legal system and meted out its own rough justice in brawls. When I visited the place in 2009 it had long ago declined and was now not much more than a sleepy highway intersection, but I found a small museum in the old railroad station where the local curator, Candace Blume, told me "most leaders of towns want to tell visitors what wonderful and good places they live in; we want to tell people how bad we are. We are the hellhole of the Middle West."

At the end of the nineteenth and beginning of the twentieth centuries Seney earned its notoriety by being the collecting point for lumberjacks, ruffians, prostitutes, rapacious merchants, and saloon keepers from all over the Midwest. Men went to Seney to get away from authorities "down below" where they often had criminal records. Many were unschooled. Most were hard drinkers. During the winters the lumberjacks were at work in the pine forests surrounding the town. Teamsters brought the logs by sledges on the ice and snow to the rivers and railway. When spring came, getting the logs out of the woods became much more difficult and therefore the camps usually suspended work until the fall. In the spring the released and restless men flooded into the town where they quickly spent their newly-received pay on liquor and women.

Logs and sledge on an iced road. Reproduced with permission of Superior View Studio

Fights were everyday events. The men often sought brawls, shouting in the streets that they could "lick any man in town." One of them, a man known as "Fighting Jim," swaggered down the plank sidewalks and anyone who did not give way was already in trouble. When a fight developed a circle of onlookers gathered around the struggling protagonists shouting "may the best man win" and eagerly followed the battle. Interference was considered improper. Although knives and guns were rarely used, the fisticuffs could be brutal, resulting often in bloodied faces and broken bones. No holds were barred, and occasionally one fighter would bite off the ear of another, or crush his face with his hobnailed boot, leaving his victim scarred with what was called "lumberjack smallpox."

Seney had a collection of characters known for their rough reputations and storied pasts. P. K. Small, better known as "Snag Jaw," was a repugnant man who rarely washed or changed his clothes, and possessed no nose, having lost it in a biting match. Devoted to chomping, he earned drinks

Munising being built in the 1890s. Photo courtesy of Alger Historical Society

by biting off the heads of snakes and frogs. "Stub Foot" O'Donnell and "Pump Handle" Joe were giant men past their primes as lumberjacks who specialized in meeting the trains when they pulled into the Seney station. The two men would get on each side of an arriving "city dude," suddenly lift him into the air, turn him upside down, and shake all the money out of his pockets. If the victim did not cause a fight Stub Foot and Pump Handle would invite him into a saloon to have a drink with the money they had just removed from him. "Frying Pan Mag" was a whore who kept an iron skillet beside her in case one of her customers caused trouble. If necessary, she brought the skillet down on the head of her unruly client. It is said that once she swung a little too hard and killed her paramour, but no one thought of locking her up since the incident was thought to be a case of self-defense.

Munising, about thirty-five miles westward from Seney and the nearest town to Grand Island, was perhaps not as rough as Seney at the end of the nineteenth and the beginning of the twentieth centuries but it too was

The expression on the faces of the men in the boat show devil may care attitudes the loggers often assumed. Reproduced with permission of Superior View Studio.

a sharp-edged and unforgiving place. It was incorporated as a village only in 1896, three years after George Genry became keeper of the lighthouse to the north of the settlement, out in the lake. Just a few sidewalks existed in the town, and they were made of wood. The town's rough culture was more variegated than that of Seney, since in addition to lumberjacks it had sailors and fishermen on the big lake where it was a port. Like Seney, it had its saloons and bawdy houses. One of the best known of its palaces of physical pleasure was a whorehouse a few miles out of town, south of Cox Pond, that could be reached only by boat. The proprietors scrutinized

Seney Belle. Reproduced with permission of Superior View Studio

Mill-worker houses built by companies in the town to almost identical design, some of which can still be seen. Photo by Loren Graham

each arriving boat for signs that it was piloted by one of their employees, ensuring protection from a rare visit by the police.

No highways connected Munising to the outside world in 1908, only rutted wagon trails., and, several miles away, a railroad junction. The need for much better roads was just being felt; the first automobile arrived by lake boat to nearby Grand Marais in the spring of 1908, a "red devil" Cadillac with a one-cylinder engine, but there was no way it could be driven to the county seat, Munising. Its owner, Roy Hewitt, showed it off in town and then shipped it out by boat, finding it of little use. The first automobile in Munising, a Model 10 Buick, was purchased in 1909 by the local railroad manager Marcus A. Doty. (Doty also owned the motor launch "Lyle D," which allegedly brought George Genry's body back to Munising on July 17, 1908.) In the winter Munising was blanketed by very heavy snow produced by the lake effect, on average over 12 feet each year. With only horses for road work, the snow was not removed from the streets, but packed down by horse-drawn rollers known as "snow pankers"; as a result a person entering a store in February would have to descend several feet from atop the snow-covered street level to the door sill of the store. Electricity supposedly arrived in 1897 but for many years most homes continued to be lighted by kerosene lamps. (Powell's Point, a mile out of town and just opposite Grand Island, did not get electricity until the 1950's, and some homes in the area, including two in my family, still do not have grid electricity today, over a century after the arrival of electrical power in town.) A telephone system, which technically also arrived in 1897, was similarly underutilized; in 1908 there were only about a hundred telephone subscribers, all within the town limits. The main town activities were logging, leather tanning, paper-making, and the manufacture of wood products such as barrels and boards. Along the shore of Munising Bay were more than a dozen mills: lumber mills, shingle mills, stave mills and cooperages.

The mills in the town and surrounding areas created mountains of wood waste which were the fuel for frequent fires, some of them devastating. In 1902 a fire started near Seney, moved to Grand Marais and then toward Munising, destroying everything on an almost forty mile path. The next year, 1903, the timbered area south of neighboring Wetmore burned so intensely that the railroad rails which crossed the area were curled into hoops. In 1908, the year of the disappearance of the lighthouse keepers, the forest near Miner's Beach, in easy sight of Grand Island, was burned bare for several miles.

The population of the Munising area was almost entirely blue collar, and most of the residents did not have a high school education, although there was a handful of lawyers and doctors, some of them with dubious professional preparation. In contrast to other nearby towns such as Escanaba, Calumet, and Marquette, Munising had almost no wealthy people, certainly no local capitalists. It was a town ruled by absentee landlords, as indicated by mill-worker houses built by companies in the town to almost identical design, some of which can still be seen.

In 1908 Munising was celebrated as a hard-drinking lumberjack town. At one point it was described as boasting "the largest liquor consumption per capita of any American city."[2] The town had 19 saloons, one for about every 130 people. The town fathers were so worried about the large number

2   Richard M. Dorson, *Blood Stoppers and Bear-Walkers: Folk tales of Immigrants, Lumberjacks & Indians,* Harvard University Press, Cambridge and London, 1952, p. 152.

of drinking establishments that in 1897 they set a limit of 20 on the number of saloons "until the population reached 10,000," a level never attained. In 1906 a local amateur sociologist made a survey that showed that on the previous Sunday 685 men attended church in Munising but that on the same

Reproduced with permission of Marquette County Historical Society

day 1087 men were counted in the local saloons. Sometimes the drinking led to riots and social disorder and economic losses to the community. After one particularly bad week, the local newspaper, the *Munising News,* gave the following report:

> Only about 25 percent of the employees of the city's largest mill are at work this week which means that the plant has shut down for the time being as the small force now on the job is employed in making repairs and there is not actual production ... Last week– after pay day– a number of the men began a grand carouse and on Saturday a considerable part of the seventy decided, without giving any previous warning, that they would not work except under conditions which the company could not accept ...Manager Stewart unhesitatingly lays (the

blame) at the doors of certain saloon men whom he says have sold intoxicants indiscriminately, without limit, and largely in excess of the quantity the law permits them to sell to any individual at any one time.

Other heads of local plants claim to be suffering from the same cause. They bitterly complain that men on their way to work are sold intoxicants before seven o'clock in the morning in direct violation of the law and in not a few cases by nine o'clock the men are unfit for work.

The population of the Upper Peninsula in the early twentieth century was seventy-five percent foreign-born. In addition to the native-born Chippewa, the loggers, fishermen, hunters, mill workers, leather workers, and shop keepers of Munising in the first decade of the twentieth century came from a variety of ethnic backgrounds: they included French-Canadians, Finns, Slovenians, Swedes, Cornishmen, Welsh, Germans, Irish, Swiss, Poles, Russians, and a few Jews. Some of their names, reflecting the richness of their ethnic origins, can still be found in Munising today: St. Amour, Clark, Riihimaa, Powell, Matson, Marks, St. Martin, Carlson, Steinhoff, Revord, Frechette, Gagnon, Des Jardins, O'Boyle, Putvin, Lezotte, LeVeque, Belfry, Cota, Bowerman, Carmody, Van Landschoot, Gollinger, Jurinen, Sullivan, Gurski, Nikkari, Miron, Wolkoff.

This resplendent ethnic mix gave birth in Munising to a folklore culture made up of people who loved to tell tall tales. Often the sagas they related had roots in the folkways of the countries of their birth, usually European but also native American. Thus, local Chippewa talked of "Bloodstoppers" and "Bearwalkers." The first were Chippewa who had the ability to stop the bleeding of a wound by issuing an incantation. The second were Chippewa who took on the form of an animal, often a bear, and had the power to cure disease or cause death. The French-Canadians in town told of the "loup-garou," (werewolf) a person possessed of the devil who must be struck with a knife in order to be rescued. Cornishmen, who worked in the mines and brought the dough-enclosed meal known as a "pasty" to the Upper Peninsula, spoke of witchcraft and omens. They also loved their whiskey, singing:

When I'm dead and in my grave
No more whiskey shall I crave
And on my tombstone let this be wrote,
Ten thousand gallons run down my throat.

The Finns regaled their listeners with stories of their "noitas," who were wizards and had the power to defend people against their enemies (such as the Russians, always on the Finnish mind). The Russians, on their part, admired the pellucid water of Lake Superior and maintained they could hear at night the chiming bells of the submerged "lost city of Kitezh," celebrated in their folklore (and opera). For lumberjacks, the more extravagant the yarn the better, and many of their stories were brutish. One would approach women with babies on the street and say "I am Jake the lumberjack, a man-eater. I haven't eaten a man in quite a while, I guess I'll have lunch." And he would open his mouth and lunge at the baby. Mothers would faint.

Miners would tell jokes to relieve the tension brought by constant threat of death in the shafts. One miner, a disagreeable chap, was struck by a falling piece of rock. A doctor was called. One of the miners asked, "Doc, is there any hope?" The doctor replied,"he isn't hurt so bad, he'll survive." The other miner replied, "No, I meant is there any hope of him dying."

Lakemen had their own stories. Captain Benjamin Truedell of the Life Saving Station in Grand Marais (the same man who gave the first report on the condition of the body of the assistant keeper Morrison of Old North Lighthouse) maintained that whenever anything important happened, he had a dream of it the night before. He told of finding bodies on the beach who, when he rolled them over, struck his hand with their hand and revealed the countenances of visitations of the previous evening.

Fishermen spoke of monsters in the lake. Angus Steinhoff and Ed Van Dein (Van Dein, as we will see, was described by the Genry family as the discoverer of George Genry's body) maintained that a monster lived in Trout Bay on Grand Island. It had, they said, "an angled head, looked like a big snake or serpent, made quite a wake…[it] zigzagged back and forth, and part of it stuck out of the water."

No story existed, it seemed, that was not amenable of embellishment. And nothing was as it seemed at first glance.

The richness of Munising folklore lasted for many decades and attracted the attention of ethnologists and anthropologists. In the summer of 1938 the (soon-to-be) famous folklorist Alan Lomax came to Munising as a twenty-three-year-old and recorded the songs of lumberjacks. (My wife, a three-year-old, was on nearby Grand Island at the time).

Lomax was sent to the Upper Peninsula by his supervisor at the Library of Congress, Harold Spivache, who was Chief of the Music Division. In these Great Depression years Lomax's salary was both modest and irregularly delivered. On September 12, 1938, Lomax pleaded with Spivache in a telegram, "Please send my advance or voucher or something. I'm not eating."[3] Lomax was on his way to Munising at the time and someone there must have fed him because he continued working. On September 28 he again wired Spivache "Am getting such grand stuff can't afford to leave. Can you wire me my salary or advance?"

The correspondence between Spivache and Lomax reveals two strikingly different approaches to the task of collecting the folklore of America. Spivache was as enthusiastic about the project as Lomax was, but Spivache was a bureaucrat who wanted accountability, prompt reports, and order. Lomax was a young bohemian kid (the FBI, suspicious of Lomax's political views, noted that he was "slovenly in his dress and appearance") who knew that he would not get the recordings he wanted if he simply went up to a lumberjack or a lakeman, stuck a recorder in front of him, and said "sing." Lomax understood that he had to establish a relationship with these original characters, which meant drinking with them, carousing with them, and sometimes even bribing them. Lomax would disappear for days, even weeks, at a time, and Spivache would send him frantic telegrams asking "Where are you? What are you doing? Where are your latest reports? I don't even have an address for you." Lomax in reply was constantly asking for money, not only for himself, but also (although he could not tell Spivache this) for all the drinks, entertainment and bribes he was paying for

---

3   AFC 1939/007 AFS 2237-2486

Alan Lomax, one of the great field collectors of folklore in America. In 1938 he came to Munising and recorded lumberjack songs now preserved in the Library of Congress. Courtesy of the Library of Congress.

in order to get his recordings. His pleas for more money to Spivache were not helped by the fact that on one occasion in Michigan while Lomax was drinking with his friends someone stole his recording equipment. Lomax traveled in an old Ford pickup truck which he had equipped as a "studio" but also as his living quarters, complete with tent and sleeping bag in case no one offered him a room.[4]

The recording equipment that Lomax had in his pickup truck was a direct-to-disk recorder called "Presto." It operated at 78 rpm and had a cantankerous stylus that etched the music onto a single acetate disk. If Lomax could not find a nearby electrical outlet he could try to power the contraption with a hand crank. While the UP loggers, sailors, and miners sang their folk songs Lomax crouched beside the Presto with a small brush about a half-inch wide in his hand which he used to brush away the little black balls of acetate chaff being produced by the stylus. If the black threads accumulated in the grooves the stylus failed to do its job properly. Sometimes Lomax was ambidextrously busy brushing chaff with one hand and cranking the power handle with the other while trying with his body to keep the whole apparatus steady. It was a tedious task even when he was sober and if not done in exactly the right and timely way the recording was slightly or even not so slightly distorted. As one listens today in the Library of Congress to Lomax's recordings of UP balladeers one becomes used to fluctuations and wails occasionally interrupting the strikingly melodious voices from an era long past.

The lumberjacks in the Upper Peninsula sang for Lomax about generational conflict, e.g. ("The Black Sheep"), religious differences, e.g. ("The Protestant Cow"), and unrequited love, e.g. ("The Bachelor's Lay"). One former lumberjack in Munising who particularly attracted Lomax's attention was the 62-year-old John Leonard, a man with a soft and mellifluous singing voice that can still be enjoyed today.[5] Leonard's own background was striking, and added one more dollop of cultural diversity to the Munising scene. Among his ancestors were both fugitive black slaves and Michigan Chippewa. Before the Civil War a number of

4   Alec Witkinson, "Take One: Presto," *The New Yorker*, April 9, 2012, p. 25.
5   Archive of Folk Culture, Library of Congress, AFS 2355-2360, LWO 4872, reel 152A.

slaves fled the American South and went to Canada. After the emancipation some of them returned to the United States and settled near Mt. Pleasant, Michigan, in Isabella County. They then often intermarried with Chippewa (there is still a Chippewa reservation in the county) and became farmers and lumberjacks. Leonard was born there around 1876 to parents whom he described to Lomax as "mulattoes." He began working at the age of 12 and at 15 he moved to the lumber camps of the Upper Peninsula, especially around Trout Lake, Seney, and Munising. Although he was little educated and spoke ungrammatically he had an innate musical sense and an ability to pick up the songs of his fellow lumberjacks, embellish them, and invent his own. He soon became popular in the bunkhouses of the camps, where he often provided the entertainment of the evenings.

Then, after World War II, the recent Harvard Ph.D. folklorist Richard Dorson came to the Upper Peninsula. Of all the towns in the U. P. that Dorson visited he reported that Munising was the most fertile in terms of legends and stories. What he found there, he wrote, "exhilarated and astonished me. The bards and troubadours of Homer's day and King Arthur's court were all there, reciting in a variety of American accents their wondrous sagas."[6] He ensconced himself in the sitting room of the old Victoria Hotel on Elm Street in Munising, next to where the Post Office is now located, and talked to people who wandered in. Sometimes he went across the street to the Peihl Hotel, where the Peoples State Bank parking lot is today. Another prime spot for listening to tales was the porch of the boarding house at 111 Elm Avenue–still standing today–where aged former lumberjacks, some of them crippled by their work, told Dorson about the logging camps in the Munising area and their rugged culture. Dorson gathered stories and returned home to Indiana University in Bloomington, where in the nineteen sixties I was his colleague and friend and begged him to relate it all again. Richard Dorson wrote a book about his experiences, entitled *Blood Stoppers and Bear Walkers*, which is considered a classic in American folklore.[7]

6   See Dorson Papers, Lilly Library, Indiana University, Box 55, folder 1, item 8. Also, Richard M. Dorson *Blood-Stoppers and Bear Walkers: Folktales of Immigrants, Lumberjacks, and Indians,* Harvard University Press, Cambridge and London, 1952, pp. vii-viii.
7   Richard M. Dorson, op. cit.

The peak of the logging period of Munising history came at the end of the nineteenth century and the beginning of the twentieth. In the period 1900 to 1910 the Cleveland-Cliffs Iron Company purchased large areas of land to furnish timber and charcoal for the mines that the company operated near Marquette, Ishpeming, and Negaunee. In the process it became one of the largest landowners in the Upper Peninsula. (This influence was still evident a hundred years later; in 2002 one-fourth of Alger County, land that had once belonged to Cleveland-Cliffs, was transferred in one sale to

The old boarding house at 111 Elm Street in downtown Munising, on the porch of which Richard Dorson recorded the talks of lumberjacks which ended up in his classic work on American folklore, *Blood Stoppers and Bear Walkers* (Harvard University Press).

Richard M. Dorson, Father of American Folklore, longtime professor at Indiana University, who found Munising to be the richest source of tales, songs and yarns in the Upper Peninsula. He interviewed many local lumberjacks, Chippewa, and lakesmen in the area, including Benjamin Truedell, the person who found the body of Edward Morrison.

another timber company. To get an idea of the size of territory involved, one notices that Alger County is almost as large as the state of Rhode Island.)

Cleveland-Cliffs set up temporary timber camps scattered throughout the county, most of them designated merely by numbers. Thus, Camp 47 was near Hovey Lake, Camp 46 was near the Widewaters Campground, Camp 79 was at Cookson Lake. The camps were wild places remote from the law where bootleg liquor circulated freely and brawls and fights were common. Food for the camps was often venison, and "market hunters" slaughtered thousands of deer for that purpose, selling the meat to the camps, which had their own cooks and kitchens. Hunting regulations were unknown. Sometimes logging crews were taken by boat along the south shore of Lake Superior to roadless spots where trees were being cut. The expressions on the faces of the men in such a boat pictured earlier showed the devil-may-care attitudes the loggers often assumed.

The men in the lumber camps engaged in exhausting labor, often working twelve to sixteen hours a day, for little pay. Although many of the men were uneducated, the labor was not simple but divided into a hierarchy of specialties. There was the "head push," the "filer," the "road monkey," the "walking boss," the "scaler," the "horse-skinner," the "cookee," the "swamper," the "river hog," the "tender," and, of course, the center of it all, the "jack." Foremen, the "head push" in each camp, were chosen not only for their knowledge of all details of lumbering but also for their ability to whip any person in the camp who became insubordinate. They were often enormous men, standing six and a half feet tall and with arms larger than most people's legs. A foreman who lost a battle was usually demoted and replaced by a tougher man. Foremen were the best paid persons in the camp, receiving 75 to 100 dollars a month.

The jacks who actually cut the trees took great pride in their skill with double-edged axes and cross cut saws. Each jack kept his own ax and sharpened it at night to a razor edge. Touching another jack's ax was considered a violation and could easily lead to a fracas. The logs were brought to the river banks in the winter on roads prepared by the "road monkeys." Enormous loads of logs, twelve to eighteen feet long, weighing as much as 100 tons, were pulled on sledges by prized Percheron horses which were given better care than the lumberjacks themselves. The teamsters were proud of their horses, called them by name, and often decorated them with colored plumes and medallions. Such horses cost from six to eight hundred dollars a piece, while a lumberjack could be hired for about twenty-five or thirty dollars a month. When the camps were closed down for the summer the jacks could wander off wherever they wanted, and the companies did not care for them, but the horses were put out for pasture and rest, their injuries and callouses were cared for, and they were fed well to give them energy for the coming fall.

Both the horses and jacks were engaged in dangerous work. Jacks were frequently killed by falling trees, and the "river hogs" who stood atop "burling" or spinning logs in the rivers during the spring drive were even more frequently killed when they fell from their perches and were crushed between neighboring logs. When such a jack or river hog was killed, he was usually buried on the spot, his boots placed above his otherwise anonymous grave. Unless relatives inquired, their fates usually went unreported.

Horses could also be killed. Often the loads were taken over frozen lakes where the slick ice made pulling the sledges easier for the horses, but the strength of the ice was frequently unknown. A sledge which went through the ice usually took the horses and the teamster with it. In order to ease the passage of the sledges on land the roads were sprinkled with water at night and froze into ice by morning. Horses could pull sledges with enormous loads on iced roads. But such roads brought their own dangers. When going downhill the loads could not be braked and the ponderous sledges could easily overtake the horses and crush them in surrounding ravines or against trees alongside the road. In order to try to prevent such runaways the teamsters would sprinkle sand on the ice on the downhill portions, but this preventive method did not always work. A sharp-eyed teamster would try to spot the moment an uncontrolled slide was beginning, quickly unhitch his team from the sledge, and get them and himself out of the way. Such an action taken too slowly meant that the teamster died first, crushed against his own horses.

The logging operations were competitive operations and many corners were cut in order to win out. Stealing logs was a widespread practice. The companies would buy sections of land for a few dollars an acre and then cut far beyond the boundaries of the land they purchased.

These illegal incursions into land belonging to the government or other owners (Indians were not considered owners), were called "harvesting the 'round forties'." The different companies jostled for privilege, and large companies with more employees sometimes encouraged brawls between their lumberjacks and those working for smaller companies, certain that their men would win.

"Branding" the logs was supposed to discourage their theft. Each company had its own brand burned into the ends of the large logs, such as § or **N** or **PaG** or **CCI**, but it was a simple matter for an unscrupulous logger to cut off a thin end section of the log with the brand, replace it with a different one, and burn the telltale sliver in a camp stove.

In each of the lumber camps Cleveland Cliffs granted one man the right to own and operate a store. With no other stores nearby offering competition, these small retail operations were profitable and desired concessions. One of these men was an itinerant Jewish merchant named Sam Marks who did so well that later he opened a permanent store in Munising (his name and ancient clothing advertisements can be viewed today painted on the brick wall on the south side of Superior Street at the intersection with Elm Street, the center of Munising.) When a lumberjack in one of the camps wished to buy something from the store, he charged it by showing the store keeper the little numbered brass plate, about the size of a fifty-cent piece, that he wore on his belt. The storekeeper sent the charges assigned to each plate number to the headquarters of the company near Marquette. The company then collected the monthly store bills by deducting them from the wages of the lumberjacks, which in 1908-1909 were $20 to $26 a month plus board. Once a month the company paymaster came by the camps on horseback and distributed wages in little cloth bags resembling tobacco pouches. Each pouch contained money equal to the monthly wage minus the store charges.

In order to hire more and more workers the company sent expeditions to other parts of the country on recruitment campaigns. For example, in 1906 the company brought 65 young Slovenians from Pennsylvania to its landholdings in the Upper Peninsula. They joined the French-Canadians who earlier had dominated the lumberjack trade.

The only workers who did not need to come from outside were Native Americans, the Chippewa who had lived in the area for centuries. Many of them disdained the lumber camps and tried to continue to live as hunters, fishermen, maple sugar gatherers, basket weavers, and farmers. At first the Chippewa, a band of about 150, lived on Munising Bay, near where the Washington School is now located, but later many of them moved about three miles east of the bay to an area first known as Thomasville, and, later, as Indiantown (as it is known today). Most of the Chippewa families had by this time assumed Anglicized names, assigned to them by a local white storekeeper, W. A. Cox, in order to simplify his bookkeeping. Common names in Indiantown in 1908 were Ames, Bird, Blair, Blake, Brown, Clark, Marshall, Sky, Thomas, and Walker. At least one native family refused to accept a new Anglicized name or the white men's ways, holding on to its Chippewa name of Kishketog. A member of this family, "Jimmy" Kishketog (Kesh-ke-tuhwug, Kishketahwaug), ignored Christianity, holding on to his Chippewa nature beliefs. He worked for nobody, and lived by hunting and fishing. He was a close friend of the lighthouse keeper George Genry, a fellow Chippewa, and together the two men often hunted on Grand Island.

When I first came to Munising in the 1950's there were still people there who remembered what the area was like at the turn of the century. Tony Lezotte, tug-boat captain and former mayor of Munising, told me that when he was a boy living in Brown's Addition the town was a place where lumberjacks ruled, men who placed premium on nonchalant masculinity and who could display tenderness, incredible sturdiness, and occasional brutality. One of the friends of his family was a logger who, while felling a tree in the nearby forest, tripped at a fatal moment and was crushed under a tree that he had cut. His friends took him to the local hospital at the south end of Maple Street, where he was put to die. Tony went to see the stricken logger with his parents. The patient was lying in the hospital bed seemingly unconscious, but when Tony and his parents entered the room he roused himself and pushed his head and shoulders up high on the pillow. The sudden movement caused blood from his crushed chest to surge up through his throat and gush out his mouth, down his neck and onto his chest,

Tony Lezotte, tug-boat captain and former mayor of Munising, who told me about the lumberjack culture of Munising in the early twentieth century.

quickly staining the sheets. The boy Tony was horrified, and asked "Is there anything we can do for you?" The half-paralyzed logger grunted "Get me a bottle of whiskey." Tony and his parents went out, bought the whiskey, and returned. The logger raised the bottle to his lips, drank half of it, and collapsed. That night he died. Tony's observation decades later was "Those guys gave toughness a new meaning."

In the early years of the twentieth century the dominant culture around Munising was that of the lumberjacks, but other groups, some old, some new, were challenging that culture and offering different visions of who should rule. They included the native Chippewa (who looked on all others as intruders), local and federal government officials (who wanted to introduce rules and order), and Eastern mining and timber businessmen (who sought to extract profits without local troubles while at the same time enjoying their privileges). Each of these groups would look at the disappearance of the lighthouse keepers from its own perspective and find a different explanation.

William G. Mather

CHAPTER IV

MARQUETTE AND WILLIAM G. MATHER

The city of Marquette, the largest metropolis of the UP today, developed along very different lines than Seney and Munising. At first Marquette was also a tough place, a frontier town founded in 1849 by a group of men including Amos Harlow, Robert Graveraet and the young Peter White. At first the settlement was called "Worcester" after the Massachusetts hometown of Harlow, but a few years later it was renamed "Marquette" in honor of the seventeenth century priest who is supposed to have visited and preached there.

Peter White later became one of the area's most prominent citizens. He was both a shrewd businessman who knew how to best his competitors and also a philanthropist who gave much to the city of Marquette. In his later life he was somewhat rotund, wore vest and gold chain, and looked like the cartoon-caricature of a wealthy businessman, but in his youth he was exceptionally virile. He delivered mail on snowshoes over hundreds of miles, traveling along forest trails. When he was elected to the Michigan state assembly in 1856 there were still no railroads or even other good roads in the Upper Peninsula, so White decided to walk to the state capital in Lansing to attend the legislative meetings, a hike of about 400 miles. When he arrived in the chamber he was greeted with a standing ovation.

Marquette was destined to be the main port for the iron ore discovered some eleven miles inland and rather quickly developed its own commercial, legal, and cultural institutions. A few of the early settlers became wealthy, including the lawyer-banker-politician White, the mining investor Edward Breitung, the clothing merchant Sam Kaufman, and the land investors Horatio Seymour, Jr., and John Longyear. These men not only prospered financially, but also launched libraries, schools, and social clubs. Several of them built palatial homes in Marquette.

They rivaled each other for social eminence. The Kaufmans, although quite wealthy, were excluded from elite organizations because they were Jewish and because the family patriarch, Samuel, married a woman of Native American descent whom some locals derisively called a "half-breed." When Seymour, Longyear, and White promoted an exclusive membership organization that later became the "Huron Mountain Club," Kaufman was not invited to join. (His son Louis, even more wealthy, was also excluded from the club and eventually built an enormous mansion and estate, Granot Loma, that was supposed to outshine the Huron Mountain Club. It had 70 rooms, over 30 fireplaces and was surrounded by 40,000 acres.)

The original name of the Huron Mountain Club was the "Huron Mountain Shooting and Fishing Club." It was established in 1889 by twelve men, four of whom were from Marquette. The land of the Club, greatly expanded over the years, was a beautiful wilderness area abutting Lake Superior with hills that amounted to small mountains and studded with crystalline lakes The founders thought of Marquette as a backward area populated by common people with whom they did not wish to associate socially. They wanted to create a summer resort area to which a chosen few from Marquette, Detroit, and Chicago could come to hunt and shoot.

The Huron Mountain Club still exists today and its thousands of acres of forest are one of the largest wilderness areas in the Middle West. The private security guards who protect it, the exclusive membership, and the admission of outsiders only by invitation have all given it a certain mystique, contributing to much gossip. Many of the memberships have remained in the same families for several generations. In private conversations one person familiar with the Huron Mountain Club told me that in its first one-hundred years no Jews were admitted, but another disputed this. At any rate, it had a reputation for not being receptive to Jews.

When William G. Mather became president of the Cleveland-Cliffs Iron Company in 1890 (a position he would hold for 50 years) he rather quickly became one of the most powerful men to frequent the Marquette arca. The question naturally arose, would he become a member of the Huron Mountain Shooting and Fishing Club, the most exclusive social organization in the Upper Peninsula? By privilege, wealth, and family ancestry he seemed eminently qualified, since he was a descendant of one of America's earliest white families of colonial Massachusetts, including the famous Puritan ministers Increase and Cotton Mather. His ancestors included many prominent people, including a president of Harvard. Yet he was not a member of the Chicago, Detroit, and Marquette cliques that dominated the club, and he had a reputation of wanting to run any organization of which he was a part. The leaders of the club feared his dominance if they let him in. For several years the issue festered while they dithered.

Mather lost his patience and decided that he would create his own wilderness utopia, and one larger and more beautiful than the Huron Mountain Club. His eyes fell on Grand Island, a 13,000 acre realm of virgin forests, colored cliffs, fish-filled lakes, and sand beaches. In 1900 he purchased it. When he asked his lawyers to form a hunting and fishing club similar to that of the Huron Mountains, but one he would run, they gave him the unfortunate news that the state of Michigan had recently passed a law prohibiting "hunting and fishing clubs over twelve and a half acres."[1] The Huron Mountain Club was not subject to this restriction because it had been founded before the law passed. The irritated Mather told his lawyers to find another way to accomplish his goals; complying, they informed him that "game preserves" were not restricted by the new law, only hunting and fishing clubs. At first Mather was displeased, saying that he wanted to hunt and fish on the island. The lawyers said that as president of the company owning the island he and his guests could hunt and fish all they wanted, but for all others it was a game preserve where such activities were prohibited. To Mather, this was a perfect situation.

The fate and shape of Grand Island in 1908, when the keeper and assistant keeper of North Light on the island disappeared, were thus tightly linked to one man, William G. Mather. His personality and his wishes became paramount. The fact that local Chippewa were accustomed

---

1   Much information on these events, especially as related to the Huron Mountain Club, can be found in C. Fred Rydholm, *Superior Heartland*: A Backwoods History, Vols. I-II, Topwater Productions, Marquette, 2006.

to hunting on the island, and thought they had treaty rights to do so, was irrelevant.

Mather was impressed with the beauty of Grand Island and he wanted to preserve it. At the same time that he was developing his dream of a forest utopia on the island he was also, back in his home of Cleveland, building a palatial mansion on a large estate on the south shore of Lake Erie with formal gardens, greenhouses, and antique furniture imported from Europe. He hired famous architects and garden designers, Charles A. Platt and Warren H. Manning, to design his Cleveland estate of several hundred acres (it was actually in Bratenahl, a suburb).

Gwinn, William Mather's Estate in Bratenahl, near Cleveland.
Courtesy of Cleveland Historical Organization

He shuttled between his pet projects, almost 600 miles apart, in a private railway car, the last part of the journey on a railroad that he also owned. The two projects were totally different in appearance and spirit, but both were clearly the creations of Mather. At his estate near Cleveland he affected the architectural and aristocratic culture he had seen during a youthful year spent in Europe (he called for "French and Italian sentiment"), but on Grand Island he aimed for comfortable wilderness on an American frontier model. He lived on the island in an immense log cabin with moose heads and stuffed animals on the walls; it was surrounded with a faux fort log stockade, as depicted below:

Photo courtesy of Alger County Historical Society

In his sylvan retreat he entertained his wealthy associates with game hunts permitted to no one else. He hired a game keeper, J. J. Murray, to attend to his wild animals, and built for him a game-keeper's lodge in an attractive rustic motif. It was Murray who would identify the body of E. S. Morrison, assistant keeper of North Light.

Game-keeper's Lodge, Grand Island
Photo courtesy of Alger County Historical Society

Mather was a man whose complex personality no one has adequately explored, at least not in writing. He was proud of his colonial ancestors and collected their writings in hundreds of volumes.

Mather's diaries, which have been preserved by the Western Reserve Historical Society in Cleveland, reveal a very private man who often treated others aloofly, even his own mother. In his diary of August 7, 1908, he admitted that he often wounded his mother's "sympathetic and loving nature by coldness." Perhaps out of guilt he decided to name after her his new lakeside estate near Cleveland "Gwinn" (her full name was Elizabeth Lucy Gwinn).

Mather's relationship with women was a mystery. In the evenings he usually dined with male business associates, or, if they were not around, alone, or with his half-sister Kate (Katherine Livingston Mather), who lived with him for many years. He was a bachelor for most of his life, marrying only at age 72, and then to a wealthy widow who was 34 years younger than he, and who lived in a lakeshore estate neighboring his in Ohio. He had a small door installed in the wall separating their estates so that he could privately visit her.

In his diaries his patrician attitude clearly emerges. He never wrote down the names of the servants, grounds keepers, boat captains, waiters, stewards, stenographers, and other employees of lower station he met and directed. He often recorded the names of his business associates who traveled with him in his private railway car, but never those who attended him. When he visited North Light on Grand Island, as his diary indicates he did several times, he did not mention that there were people living there, the keeper (George Genry) and his family, as well as the assistant keeper. Yet there was one important exception to his failure to pay attention in his diaries to people socially beneath him, and it is revealing, even touching: in the back pages of his diaries he recorded the names, dates, and causes of deaths of his workers who died in mining accidents, of whom there were distressingly many. Mather remarked that the miners he employed had to do dirty and dangerous work. He lamented and criticized the "saloon

The gate many years later. Photo taken by Loren Graham

keepers" who preyed upon them and he tried, unsuccessfully, to keep his workers away from their establishments. He attempted to reduce the death rate among his workers through safety measures, and he pioneered in the creation of worker communities with social benefits that, even though meager, were advanced for the time. One of those towns in the Upper Peninsula he named for his mother shortly after her death in 1908, just as he did his Cleveland estate. It is called today "Gwinn, Michigan" and is on the National Register of Historic Places as a "Model Town."

Mather was active in many philanthropies. He was, or became, a trustee of Trinity College, Western Reserve University (which, as Case Western Reserve University, contains even today "Mather College"), Kenyon College, University Hospitals in Cleveland, and the Cleveland Museum of Art. He gave a chapel to his alma mater in Connecticut, Trinity College. He was proud of the fact that his family had produced dozens of ministers; he eventually donated his extensive collection of their writings to the University of Virginia, where it resides in a special "Mather Collection." He was active in the Episcopal Church, attended services almost every Sunday, and usually recorded in his diaries the name of the minister who preached the sermon, even though he said nothing about the content of the discourse. Mather's name is still well-known in Cleveland, and a ship named after him is a museum in the center of the city.

Thus, Mather, like Alexander Agassiz, combined in his personality contradictory traits not uncommon among industrial tycoons of the late nineteenth and early twentieth centuries, such as Andrew Carnegie and John D. Rockefeller. On the one hand, he could be merciless in his business dealings, relentlessly pursuing his debtors, eliminating his competitors, and praising to the lower officers of his company the necessity of being "firm." On the other hand, he was generous in his selected philanthropies and he enjoyed being known as a benefactor and social leader, especially in his native Cleveland, but also in the Upper Peninsula of Michigan. He lamented the low level of education and culture in Munising, the nearest settlement to Grand Island, and he financed a high school, Mather High, that still exists today, although now devoted to the lower grades. He also created two resort hotels in or near the town, the Beach Inn in Munising, and Williams Hotel on Grand Island. After dining in relative splendor in the new Beach Inn, Mather recorded in his diary that "Munising is improving."

Mather had prominent friends interested in conservation, including Steven J. Mather (a distant cousin), the first director of the National Park Service, and Gifford Pinchot, of the U. S. Forest Service and governor of Pennsylvania. Following their advice, he went to great lengths to preserve the forests and wildlife on the island. He spoke of creating on the island what he called "A Second Yellowstone Park." He showed off brochures describing the island to his friends, the cover of one of which is illustrated below.

Photo courtesy of Superior View Studio

Mather allowed virtually no logging of the largely virgin forests and he sharply restricted visitors and vehicles. However, he often invited his friends to hunt, including Carter H. Harrison, mayor of Chicago, Chase Osborn, governor of Michigan, and Oscar Mayer, the meat-packing mogul. Both Harrison and Mayer wrote their names on the walls of their hunting cabins, where they can still be seen today.

Mather was an avid preservationist, but he practiced a form of wildlife management that violated the accepted rules of today. He ordered his men to bring in many exotic species of animals and plants that were not adapted to the area – reindeer from Finland, elk from lower Michigan, brush hare from England, grouse from Sweden and Scotland, and American caribou, antelope, and moose. Deer were already in abundance. He also supervised the planting of Scotch Pine, cranberries, and wild flowers. The importation project was largely a failure, although some of the types of animals survived for decades, and some of the birds and plants are still there. Many of the animals died out in the winter of 1902-1903. Simultaneously with his introduction of alien species Mather tried to eliminate the native predators. At great expense he organized expeditions of several dozen men who hunted down and eliminated the wolves. One of the results was that the remaining deer and moose were not culled in a natural way, and disease, especially brain worm among the moose, was common

Mather created an idyllic wildlife utopia on Grand Island. However, one feature of the island came to irritate him more and more: he did not own quite all of it, just about ninety-eight percent of it. Two lighthouse lots, totaling several hundred acres, belonged to the U.S. government. These "foreign" pieces of land were areas where "Indians" like George Genry, Timothy Dee, and Jimmy Kishketog could live on the island over Mather's opposition and shoot his wildlife..

In 1908 tourism was not yet significant as an economic factor in the Munising area. However, largely as a result of William Mather's influence, a few outsiders with very different social and economic outlooks from the rough lumberjacks who ruled the town were beginning occasionally to come to the area. The new hotels which he sponsored in the early part of the century—the Beach Inn on the mainland and Hotel Williams on the south end of the island -- brought a new style of life to grubby Munising, and they also introduced social tensions between outsiders and insiders, between the relatively wealthy visitors, and the much poorer local residents. These newcomers demanded superior services. The arrival of the outsiders, the men wearing ties and the women fine dresses not known to the local inhabitants, is pictured below:

Courtesy of Superior View Studio

One of Mather's Pronghorn antelopes at the Murray Bay dock. Courtesy of Alger County Historical Society

The new hotels had special back rooms for the servants who came with the guests but were not permitted to dine in the hotel dining room. The company sometimes held meetings of its board of directors in these hotels, and the officers, many of them from Cleveland and other eastern cities, feasted at linen-covered tables served by local residents. The cost of staying at the Beach Inn or Hotel Williams greatly exceeded the possibilities of most Munising citizens. The guests of the hotel on Grand Island were transported to the island from town in Cleveland Cliff's boats flying the flag of the company, as shown below.

Courtesy of Alger County Historical Society

The company's supervisors emphasized their social and economic superiority to the local workers by the way they dressed and acted. On Grand Island the company established a maple sugar camp, taking over the traditional camp of the local Chippewa. The following photograph shows one of the supervisors (dressed in coat and tie) directing men of simpler attire who labored with horses and sledges to bring the maple sap to the boiling vats of the sugar camp.

Courtesy of Alger County Historical Society

The year before George Genry and Edward Morrison disappeared from North Light the Hotel Williams on the south end of the island introduced a horse carriage tour service for visitors to the island. Mather had recently built a road that went up the west side of the island all the way to the lighthouse on the north end. This arrival of tourists at the lighthouse was a totally new development, and it had massive impact.

A photograph of the carriage with ladies in fancy hats. Courtesy of Alger County Historical Society

For decades before, and during the previous 14 years of George Genry's tenure as keeper in the lighthouse, it had been a place of almost total isolation, reached only with great difficulty. Genry did what he wanted, when he wanted, and he did not worry about the outside world's opinions of him, nor the regulations of white authorities. Now, a carriage would periodically pull up in his backyard, filled with tourists who wanted to gawk at him and his lighthouse. They treated George and his family as stage props, and asked to be photographed together with them in front of the lighthouse.

George was not pleased. His children, however, were fascinated. Little Johanna (named after her mother), nine years old, decided that the arrival of these hotel guests was a business opportunity. With the help of her mother, she made lemonade and iced tea which she offered to the newcomers for a nickel a glass. The tourists were delighted to see the cute lightkeeper's daughter with her refreshment stand in the backyard, and they almost all purchased lemonade. Johanna suddenly had a little income all of her own. She would tell me about it seventy years later and search for her lost nickels.

CHAPTER V

LIGHTHOUSES, IN GENERAL AND ON GRAND ISLAND

ighthouses were obviously needed by the United States, with its extensive shoreline, as they were by all maritime nations. But who should run them? The administration of lighthouses is a subject all of its own. Most people in the United States, if they know anything about lighthouses, assume that the U.S. government administers them and that they are in the custody of the U.S. Coast Guard. However, lighthouses in the U.S have been under the Coast Guard only since 1939, long after the events described in this book.

In the United States the first lighthouses were established, as was sometimes the case in Europe, not by governments but by local people, usually merchants. In Boston, in 1713, a group of such local merchants appealed to the colonial government to pay for a lighthouse for the harbor. The government agreed, and in 1715 America's first official lighthouse was established on Little Brewster Island in Boston harbor, paid for by dues levied on entering ships. (It is today the only lighthouse in the U.S. still with a keeper.) Other lighthouses were established in the eighteenth century by ports and cities on the Atlantic coast.

Not until 1789 did the central government recognize its obligation to provide reliable navigational aids. In that year the U.S. Congress passed, and President George Washington signed, an act taking responsibility for lighthouses and placed them under the jurisdiction of the Treasury Department. At first, keeper appointments were approved by the president. President Thomas Jefferson wrote that "keepers should be dismissed for small degrees of remissness, because of the calamities which even these produce."[1]

---

1   National Archives, Record Group 26, Entry 17J, "Records Relating to the Library of Congress Exhibit, 1785-1852."

In 1903 the Commerce Department took control of lighthouses and thus was in charge at the time of the events described in this book. (Today the lighthouses of the United States, a dwindling number, fall under the Department of Homeland Security, of which I, a member of the Coast Guard Auxiliary and operator of a Coast Guard radio in North Light, am a founding member).

In the first half of the nineteenth century lighthouses in the United States were vastly inferior to those in Europe, especially those in Britain and France, the leading maritime nations of the time. One sea captain observed that it was useless to look for the lighthouses on American coasts because they were so poorly illuminated he would "run ashore looking for them." In France and England the lighthouses by the 1830's used the superior "Fresnel lens" but in the United States this technology was resisted for over twenty years by the senior administrator of lighthouses, Stephen Pleasonton of the Treasury Department, who had a cozy relationship with the manufacturer of an inferior type of lens.

The backwardness of U.S. lights became so obvious that in 1851 the U.S. Congress gave in to a deluge of calls for reform, and instigated an investigation that resulted in a complete change of the U.S. lighthouse establishment. The Congress established "The Lighthouse Board" for the running of the lights, still for many years under the Treasury Department, but after about 1855 under much more enlightened leadership. Joseph Henry, a distinguished scientist, and first head of the Smithsonian Institution, long was a member of the board, serving as its chairman from 1872 to 1878. The Lighthouse Board made many changes: it introduced the Fresnel lens, it experimented with various types of fuels for the lamps, and it issued detailed instructions to lighthouse keepers. It also divided the country into districts, with a Navy officer acting as inspector in each of the districts. This officer made regular inspection trips to the lighthouses, tried to ensure observation of the rules, oversaw all personnel problems, and received complaints from the keepers and assistant keepers.

Although the institution of the Lighthouse Board was an improvement over the previous system of administration of lighthouses, it did not end the policies of favoritism and political influence that always had been characteristics of lighthouse operations. Members of Congress and other high officials maneuvered, often successfully, to get relatives and favorite people appointed as keepers, sometimes a desirable position (depending on location and conditions) even though the pay was very low. One of many examples was the appointment of Harriet Colfax as keeper of the Michigan City Light Station in Indiana from 1861 to 1904; her cousin Schuyler Colfax was a member of Congress, and, under Ulysses Grant, vice-president of the United States.[2]

Actually, the appointment of Harriett Colfax as keeper of the Michigan City Light in 1861 can be viewed from two very different standpoints. On the one hand, it is an example of political influence. On the other hand, it was an unusual case of a woman achieving a non-clerical U. S. Government job at a time when that was very rare. Women were not usually appointed keepers or assistant keepers of lighthouses. The first known case was an exception to which no one objected: when the keeper of Gurnet Point Light near Plymouth, Massachusetts, joined George Washington's forces to fight in the Revolutionary War his wife Hannah took over her husband's duties. In the nineteenth century a number of trailblazing women became keepers or assistant keepers, usually when their spouses in those positions became sick or died. Between 1820 and 1851 approximately 30 widows served as keepers, at least briefly.[3] Catherine Shook at Point aux Barques lighthouse became Michigan's first female light keeper after her husband drowned in 1849. In the later nineteenth century there were more, but in the twentieth century their numbers declined again since the authorities believed women could not handle the increasingly technical demands of the job (operating and repairing fog horns and other equipment, etc.).[4] Colfax was perhaps the most striking woman keeper, since she was never married and, in fact, lived with a female companion.

---

2   For interesting details of lighthouse life see Mary Louise and Candace Clifford, "Personnel Problems Under the U.S. Light-House Board, 1852-1901," *The Keeper's Log,* XXV, No. 4, 2009, pp. 11-19; and J. Candace Clifford and Mary Louise Clifford, Nineteenth Century Lights: Historic Images of American Lighthouses, Cypress Communications, Alexandria VA, 2000.
3   Ross Holland, *Maryland Lighthouses of the Chesapeake Bay,* Maryland Historical Society Press, Crownsville, Maryland, 1997, p. 27.
4   Patricia Majher, *Ladies of the Lights: Michigan Women in the U.S. Lighthouse Service,* University of Michigan Press, Ann Arbor, 2010.

Women had difficulty becoming keepers or assistant keepers but blacks were totally excluded. It was very difficult for them even to be employed as workmen around lighthouses. A regulation issued by the Light-House Board in 1862 said that hiring Negroes, even as laborers, would require special dispensation from Washington. Francis Ross Holland, historian of U. S. lighthouses, wrote that "So far no evidence has turned up that a black man attained any position of responsibility."

Native Americans also encountered prejudice in the lighthouse service, but their situation was a little better than that of blacks. The keeper of St. Helena Lighthouse in Lake Michigan from 1901 to 1918, Joseph Fountain, was a Chippewa. Keepers at Gay Head Lighthouse in Massachusetts and Cape Hatteras in North Carolina frequently hired Native Americans as workers. Keeper Cameron at North Light on Grand Island in the eighteen seventies was, as we will see, married to a Chippewa woman and had many children who were part Native American. One of them, Frank, later served as keeper of North Light. And George Genry, the keeper of that same lighthouse who is at the center of this story, was part Chippewa. Old North Light on Grand Island had an unusual reputation as a place of Chippewa influence. Between the time of its construction in 1867 and the disappearance of its keepers in 1908 Chippewa were usually in residence in the lighthouse. In that sense they maintained the tradition of the Treaty of Washington which granted Chippewa residence and hunting rights on the island.

Many keepers had their own reasons for preferring lighthouse work, often related to personal and local circumstances. The most popular lighthouses were near cities, but some people preferred the isolated lighthouses where they could live their own life styles and engage in other activities, occasionally illegal. These activities included unusual marital and sexual combinations, charging people for admission to scenic lighthouses, running gambling houses for local residents, merchantmen, or fishermen, poaching of animals and fish, acting as shoemaker, tailor, or justice of the peace, arranging under the table business deals with merchant vessels, acting as pilots for pay for arriving vessels, brewing and distilling alcoholic beverages, and forcing assistant keepers or family members to do all the work while the keeper did something else. The keeper of the remote Farallon Island Light Station in California illegally invited men to harvest the seals on the rocks around the light and then split the proceeds with them.

The rules that were given lighthouse keepers in the U.S. were so strict and detailed that they almost invited infractions. Lighthouse keepers were told in 1835 that they were to trim the wicks every four hours during the night, were to keep everything spotlessly clean, were forbidden to leave the station without the permission of "the Superintendent," were to keep meticulous records of all supplies used, were prohibited from engaging in any "business" that interfered with their duties, and, after 1884, were instructed to wear regulation uniforms, even "brown working suits" for outdoor work. No unauthorized personnel were to touch the equipment, not even family members. Lone keepers without assistants who often did not see any authorities for months at a time frequently simply disregarded many of these regulations.

Harriet Colfax lived in the Michigan City Lighthouse for over forty years, together with her companion, Ann Hartwell. The work was shared by the two women and, by all accounts, was excellently performed. When the two women died in 1905 a journalist in the local newspaper observed that theirs had been "a life long companionship between two most worthy and esteemed maiden ladies which has had few if any equals outside of the marital state."

Homosexuality between keepers and assistant keepers on remote stations occurred, but was almost never reported or mentioned. The assistant keeper of Penfield Reef Light Station in Connecticut was a bigamist; he kept one wife in the lighthouse, another ashore.

Thus, lighthouse keepers were often idiosyncratic. Some of them sought the most isolated lights because they simply did not like to be around other people. If such a keeper was forced to live at close quarters with an assistant keeper, difficulties often arose. Sometimes the men engaged in physical altercations. One assistant keeper reported that he had been repeatedly kicked and punched by his boss, and another said the keeper threatened him with a pistol.

Isolated keepers often worked when they were deathly ill; frequently there was no other choice if the light was to continue operating. The keeper of South Manitou Light, an island station in Lake Michigan, wrote in 1892 that he was very sick, trying to keep going, and that "I think if I could get 15 days leaf (sic) I could get cured or helped. There is not enny (sic) doctor nearer than 210 miles." Several keepers were driven insane by the numbing isolation and lack of human contact.

Drinking, although prohibited by the rules, was a particular problem. In 1892 Keeper C. H. Lewes at Port Washington Light Station in Wisconsin wrote the inspector: "I have a complaint to make against my Assistant, the trouble is caused by his habit of frequenting saloons and...coming to the station considerably under the influence of liquor. When I told him . . . that he violated the rules & that such conduct could not be tolerated, he did not seem to consider it of much importance..." Firing an assistant keeper was often more of a problem than keeping a troublesome one, since replacements were hard to find because of the low pay. Keeper Chapman at a Wisconsin lighthouse wrote in 1887, "As Mr. Russell has left me I am without a laborer . . . . It is pretty hard to get any one to work for the small wages. . . . My wife is standing watch with me now as I can not get a man." In the same year the *San Francisco Chronicle* reported that the keeper of the Point Reyes Light Station in California was "notorious for his love of the flowing bowl. It is said that he regaled himself, when out of whiskey, with the alcohol furnished for cleaning lamps, and a familiar sight to the nearby ranchmen was this genial gentleman lying dead drunk by the roadside, while his horse, attached to the lighthouse wagon, grazed at will over the country."

There were, of course, numerous stories of bravery and heroism connected with lighthouses. In 1856, only one year after the first lighthouse was built at the north end of Grand Island, it was the scene of a dramatic story involving shipwreck. The ship involved was.the sidewheel steamer Superior, built in 1845 in Perrysburg, Ohio. For the first nine years of its life it operated on the lower lakes since there was no canal to Lake Superior. But the need for large vessels to serve the new mining operation near Marquette was so great that in 1854, a year before the new canal opened, the Superior was dragged overland to Lake Superior, the largest vessel ever brought in that difficult way to the uppermost lake. The Superior was a 567–ton vessel that could carry over 50 passengers.

In the fall of 1856, the Superior was making its way from the eastern end of the lake to Marquette, loaded with mining supplies, cattle, and 53 passengers, including women and children. On the evening of October 29th the vessel was caught in a heavy storm which eventually carried away the ship rudder. Helpless, it drifted toward the high cliffs near what is now called "Spray Falls" (a waterfall) about 12 miles east of the new Grand Island Lighthouse. Soon the steamer hit the rocks, its stacks were carried away, the water engulfed the ship, the boiler furnaces were extinguished, and the vessel began to break up. Darkness had fallen and the only sign of civilization that the desperate passengers could see was a flashing glimmer from the Grand Island Lighthouse. Women and children were loaded into a boat, but it swamped and the passengers were lost within minutes. Some men devised various ways of floating in the icy waters, such as holding on to doors from the cabins or other pieces of wood, and made it successfully to the rocks where they were pummeled by waves for the rest of the night.

Eventually the men repaired two boats that had washed ashore and, with great difficulty, made their way to Grand Island, where they split into two groups. One group headed along the south shore, wading in the shallow water or trudging through the snow, sixteen inches deep, toward the only settled point in the area, the old fur-trading post on the south end of the island, where the Williams and Powell families had homes. The other group headed to the north, toward the new Grand Island lighthouse. The suffering of both groups was intense, since their feet were frost-bitten. Some members of both groups eventually made it to their destinations, but quite a few dropped out and perished on the way. One of the men later described his ordeal in an article published in *The New York Daily Times:*

> The night was unusually dark and the tangled underbrush and fallen timber rendered the traveling extremely painful and difficult with our swollen feet and exhausted frames. My two companions soon fell behind, so that by 2 o'clock a.m. I heard nothing of them. I was at this time so much exhausted myself as to be unable to travel more than twenty minutes a time. Then I would sit down and nap. This I scarcely dared to do, fearing that I should be unable to proceed, should I sit too long, or perhaps, that I should not awake at all.

The total number of the original 53 who survived is much disputed in the sources, but it was probably around fifteen. About six of these made it through the snow to the Grand Island Lighthouse, where the astounded keeper gave them food and warmth. Once they were able, they had to walk through the snow for ten more miles to reach a place at the south end of the island where they were rescued by a small ship from Marquette, the *General Taylor.*

One of the early keepers of the Grand Island Lighthouse, William Cameron, was an example of those keepers who sought isolation from society because of personal circumstances. Born north of Lake Superior, in Canada, Cameron received an advanced education in Toronto in European languages and literature. He knew Latin, Greek, and several other European languages. A desired career as a scholar or teacher did not materialize, and eventually he moved to the United States, settling in Sault Ste. Marie, Michigan, which had a large native American population. Cameron, with his interest in languages and culture, became fascinated with the richness of the lore of the Chippewa, just as Henry Schoolcraft had been in the same location years earlier. Cameron fell in love with and then married a young Chippewa woman named Sophie Nolan, learned the Chippewa language, and raised a family that eventually included many children, reputedly eleven. William and Sophie always spoke Chippewa to each other, and their children grew up speaking both Chippewa and English.

William and Sophie soon ran into trouble in Sault Ste. Marie. Local whites accused William of going native, of being an "Indian-lover," and of raising half-breeds. The whole family encountered such prejudice that William decided that they must leave. He applied for a job with the U.S. Lighthouse Service and asked for assignment to an isolated post where he, his wife, and their children could lead lives away from the narrow-minded torments of others.

The Lighthouse Service obliged by assigning him to the Grand Island Light Station. At that time no town existed in the area, so the Camerons lived in the new brick lighthouse year-round, even though for months in the winter there was no ship traffic on the frozen lake. They witnessed frightful storms in which the lighthouse shuddered. On September 18, 1872, Cameron wrote in the lighthouse log "This has been without exception the most severe storm we have ever experienced since we have been in charge of this Light. The seas were so tremendous as to carry away forty three feet three inches of the stairway that leads from the landing to the top of the hill." On other occasions he was engulfed in blizzards so dense that he had to tie a string to the backdoor of the lighthouse that he held on to as he went to the outhouse, so he would not lose his way along the seventy-foot path. He also recorded tornadoes that ripped trees out by their roots and caused multiple water spouts out on the lake.

They sometimes went for months without seeing a ship or another human being. On February 28, 1874, Cameron observed, "The monotony of the place prevents me from making many remarks further than to state that the winter so far has been pleasant." In the middle of May in that year the excited Cameron sighted in the lake the first ship he had seen in six months and exuberantly wrote in the log, "Hip, hip hurrah! A propeller rounds the point, on her way up to Marquette, ploughing through the ice."

On another occasion when the loneliness of the place got to him Cameron quoted the verse:

> When friendships have withered
> And fond hopes have flown
> Oh who would inhabit
> This drear world alone?

The children were home-schooled. William installed his books in several languages in bookshelves lining the main hallway of the lighthouse leading up to the tower.

I soon found that descendants of William and Sophie still live in the Munising area, and I interviewed one of them, Julia Cameron, while doing research for this book. Julia also spoke both English and Chippewa, and sang a song in Chippewa for me about the history of the island.

All keepers of lighthouses were required to keep logs in which they recorded daily weather observations, ship sightings, and, of course, any indication of ships in distress. William Cameron dutifully fulfilled all these requirements, and in addition he inscribed in the official log his personal reactions to all events. Cameron was irrepressible in his literary ambitions and, to the consternation of the occasional inspectors of his records, he often put little essays and verses into the official log. Early one August morning Cameron wrote:

> At 2:30 a.m. a large eared owl sat perched upon the railing of the tower, as sedate and important as a Judge Advocate upon a court martial. But when the bull's eye of the Fresnel lens would flash upon him, he would throw up his wings and cast his head down, as much as to say, "I submit." But no sooner would the flash be off of him, when he would hoot – as if he called "Come on McDuff!" He finally retired to his native forest where he came upon a "brither chum" with whom he had quite a conversation. Although I am an old resident of the woods I never could learn their language thoroughly, which prevents me from committing his honor's discourse to paper.

As the sole keeper of the lighthouse Cameron could arrange his schedule as he saw fit, and in the winters there was much time for reading, writing, and educating his children. In the summers, he was much busier, since without an assistant he was required to tend the light all night.

Also each summer a ship, a lighthouse tender named the Dahlia, captained by John Hallaran, brought canned food, barrels of flour and sugar, fuel for the burner in the Fresnel lens, kerosene for reading lamps, and coal for the stoves. Sometimes Captain Hallaran also brought what was known as the "Lighthouse Library," a box of circulating books. Each allotment of books was delivered in a special case, with an inventory of its contents on a sheet attached to the underside of the lid. To obtain a new case of books when the tender made its next visit, Cameron had to return the old case, watching the petty officer from the Dahlia carefully check each of the books against the inventory to make sure that none was missing. Cameron was critical of the books, often cheap adventure novels designed to provide some entertainment for lonely lighthouse keepers, many of whom were barely literate. He preferred his own library, but he begged the captain to bring recent works of literature, especially poetry, and children's books for his little sons and daughters. Evidently the authorities in Detroit, where the Dahlia was based, assented to some of his requests.

Just as Cameron found the books brought by the Dahlia unsatisfactory, so also he was displeased with the monotonous diet supplied by the canned goods. Whenever he could he supplemented the family larder by hunting and fishing on the island. Venison, bear meat, whitefish, trout, partridges, and many kinds of berries added variety to the lighthouse diet.

Sometimes Cameron hunted with local Chippewa, including the legendary Gashkiewisiwin-gijigong , or Powers of the Air[5], who were drawn to him by his knowledge of their language and culture. The forests of the island were free areas, with no regulations on hunting or anything else, as they had been for centuries.

As they walked among the virgin white pines Powers of the Air and the other Chippewa told Cameron of their legends and stories;

Inside this nondescript, run-down structure is one of the oldest buildings in Munising, the log church of Powers of the Air, the Native American legendary hero of Grand Island and friend of William Cameron, keeper of Old North Light. Photo by Loren Graham

they spoke of magical rope swings soaring far out over Lake Superior and built by a Grand Island Chippewa named Wawabezowin; of an enchanted canoe possessed by Mishosha that could travel at great speed if one knew the correct incantation; of giant birds that Waubewonga could make appear; of the mystical powers of Shingwauk, who once lived on Grand Island and collected a library of birch-bark books with Chippewa songs and legends.[6]

---

5   For his story, see Loren Graham, *A Face in the Rock: The Tale of a Grand Island Chippewa,* University of California Press, Berkeley, 1996.
6   In 1855, the early German ethnographer Johann Georg Kohl journeyed to meet the aged Shingwauk and see his collections; he found that Shingwauk had recently died and just before his death burned all his birch-bark documents, songs, legends, and magical symbols so that the white men would not be able to take them over. See: Johann Georg Kohl, *Kitschi-Gami: Erzählungen von Obern See*, Bremen, 1859.

Powers of the Air eventually took on an Anglicized name, Jim Clark, assigned to him by local whites, and became a lay Methodist minister. The log church in Indian Town which he built was later moved to Munising, where it is today the oldest structure in the town, but is unknown and hidden behind the anonymous wood sideboards of a decrepit house in "Frog Hollow."

The lens which Cameron attended was a fragile affair and on its base was a shiny brass plate engraved with the name of its maker, "L. Sautter, Paris." Sunlight was never allowed to strike it since the sun's rays could be refracted and magnified by the prisms in such a way that the heat could warp the glass or cause a fire. In the evening during navigation season, Cameron opened the curtains, filled the fuel reservoir (at first with whale oil, later lard oil, and later still kerosene); trimmed the wick of the lamp, polished the glass and metal reflectors, and ignited the wick. Lard oil was a particular problem because in cold weather it would solidify, and therefore had to be warmed before use. During the night he watched the flame closely, adjusting its height if necessary, trimmed the wick frequently, and often cleaned the lens and washed the windows. If ice formed on the windows he used alcohol and once – when he had exhausted the alcohol – wine to keep the focal plane of the light clear of obstructions. At dawn Cameron always extinguished the light and drew the protective curtains in the lightroom.

At night the lens revolved on clockwork machinery that caused the light to flash according to its unique pattern. The machinery was powered by pendulum weights attached to cords that descended from a brass drum in the lightroom through pulleys and then over brass sheaves into flues that extended the full length of the tower between its double brick walls. One of Cameron's duties was to wind up the pendulum weights, as if he was caring for a giant grandfather clock four stories high. If he did this at the right time and in the right way the clock mechanism would work all night without needing to be rewound, but when in December or January it was very cloudy, and the darkness lasted longer than usual, one of Cameron's challenges was to wind up the weights again without disturbing the pattern of light still being emitted. This meant cranking in the seconds between flashes, a task requiring careful coordination, with his wife often shouting out the seconds. At other times Powers of the Air volunteered to help out with tending the light. Such assistance was against the rules of the Lighthouse Establishment, which specified that "no unqualified person" was allowed to touch the equipment. This rule was frequently ignored, since family members all over the world often helped keepers out. Nonetheless, Cameron was reprimanded for this practice when it was detected by the inspector on the Dahlia. With the exception of this blemish on his record, Cameron was considered an exemplary keeper

By the end of the nineteenth century American lighthouses had come up to the best practices abroad, but they still suffered from defects. Keepers were often only semiliterate; drunkenness, dereliction of duty, and absence from the post were common offenses, despite the strict rules prohibiting all these practices. The number of lighthouses and other navigational aides increased rapidly in the last decades of the century, yet the nine-member Lighthouse Board still attempted to run all of them, being responsible even for adjudicating the complaints about the misbehavior of individual lighthouse keepers. In 1903 lighthouses were transferred from the Treasury Department to the Commerce Department in an attempt to find a more efficient administration, but problems remained. The Lighthouse Board was still in existence, and it was dominated by military officers who did not owe their allegiance either to the Treasury Department or the Commerce Department, but instead to the U.S. Army and U.S. Navy, which temporarily assigned them to the Board. Thus, the lines of authority within the Lighthouse Establishment were not clear. While the Commerce Department was, strictly speaking, responsible for lighthouses in 1908, officers from the U.S. Navy and U.S. Army made many of the important decisions. Keepers who could establish a friend or a protector on the Lighthouse Board could often escape punishment for infractions.

Munising was a port with a fine natural harbor, the only satisfactory one along a long stretch of the south shore of Lake Superior. The coastline directly east of the town was exceptionally dangerous, a long series of high cliffs offering no refuge to ships. As a result, the federal government concentrated a number of lighthouses and life-saving stations in the area. At one time between Grand Marais (40 miles east of Munising) and Au Train (seven miles west of Munising) there were eight lighthouses and two life-saving stations, employing in total approximately thirty people.[7] Today, there is not a single such employee, although seven of the lighthouses still operate on an automated basis. In 1908 the number of lighthouses was at a peak, never before or after matched. In the early fall of that year Grand Island Channel Light (South Light) was put out of service, replaced by the new Munising range lights. But in June 1908, when Genry and Morrison disappeared, all the lights were operating and had keepers, some of them had assistant keepers, and both life-saving stations had officers in charge. Most of these men became involved, in one way or another, with the events described in this book.

George Genry became keeper of the Grand Island Lighthouse in 1893 and, as a person who was part Chippewa, he continued William Cameron's and his son Frank's (also a keeper) tradition of Native American influence at the lighthouse. But Genry was a very different character than Cameron, much less educated and knowledgeable. He was similar to Cameron, though, in seeking isolated posts. Before he served in North Light on Grand Island he worked as an assistant keeper in several other remote island lighthouses in Lake Superior, many miles from the nearest settlements. He seemed to enjoy being alone except for periodic trips to towns where he drank heavily. Not sociable or devoted to his family in the way that William Cameron was, and totally uninterested in literature or worldly questions, he was a self-contained man. His few friends were often Chippewa.

---

7   The original lighthouses were: Grand Marais, Au Sable, Grand Island (North Light), Grand Island Channel (South Light), Munising North Range, Munising South Range, Grand Island West Channel North Range, Grand Island West Channel South Range, Grand Marais Life-Saving Station, and Munising (Sand Point) Life-Saving Station.

CHAPTER VI

A DRUNK AND A MURDERER?

any newspaper articles in 1908 suggested that George Genry was a drunk and a murderer, and that he had killed assistant keeper Morrison in a fight. The *Detroit Free Press*, sensing a dramatic story in this disappearance of the keepers of a lonely lighthouse, dispatched a reporter to Munising as soon as the paper learned of the discovery of Morrison's body on June 13. On June 15 the reporter sent back an article asserting that Genry had been drinking heavily for several days in Munising before starting for the lighthouse on June 6th. The reporter continued that he had found a man in Munising who swore that Genry soon returned to town after he left for the lighthouse. Three people in Munising allegedly told the reporter that they had seen Genry drinking heavily in local saloons on June 9 and 10 (three and four days after Genry made his trip to the lighthouse) and that he had then "disappeared." If true, this information was crucially important, because it indicated that Genry had survived whatever happened to Morrison and was still alive.

On June 12, 1975, I gave a talk to the Alger County Historical Society meeting in the Munising Community Center. My wife and I had only three years earlier acquired Old North Lighthouse and were busy trying to restore it. The Alger County Historical Society asked me to talk on the subject "History, Renovation, and Present-Day Living in Old North Light."

At this time I knew only a little about the events of 1908 and I mentioned them only briefly, speaking mainly about the immense restoration project in which we were engaged. I did, however, say that I had seen several newspaper articles about the disappearance of the keepers, and that several of them suggested murder. I confessed ignorance about the details of the case.

I assumed that after 67 years no one in the audience of fifty or sixty people would have any memory of the event. But as I finished my talk I noticed a very old man at the back of the room get up and start walking forward toward me. I thought, "that man looks like he may have something to say on this subject."

The man came up to me and observed,

> I was interested in what you had to say about George Genry. I knew him well, although I can't say I liked him. My name is Bill Cox. Maybe you know about Cox Chevrolet here in town; it belongs to my family. Anyway, let me tell you about George Genry. He was a whiskey-drinking son-of-a-bitch and he definitely killed Morrison. He was a skilled boatman and he could pilot a boat just fine when he was dead drunk. In fact, when he was drunk he always stood up in the boat. He was standing when he left Munising for the lighthouse that day in June, 1908. After he killed Morrison he returned to town for a couple of days --before anyone knew what had happened at the lighthouse. He was seen here in town by several people during those days. Then he fled to Canada. His wife stayed in town and was not one bit worried about the story that her husband had died. She only acted worried after the authorities got involved.

Was this a story of murder? I began exploring more thoroughly the known facts about George Genry and soon I discovered something about him that contradicted the version of events that Cox had given me: In Maple Grove Cemetery in Munising there is a tombstone for George Genry with a death date of 1908.

Furthermore, I found a July 17, 1908, story in the local newspaper, the *Munising News*, saying that Genry's body had been found on a remote beach, partially decomposed, and therefore quickly buried. How could Cox's story and that of the local newspaper be reconciled?

I went back to Cox and asked him. His reply was startling, "Oh, Genry's family just made up that story in order to cash in on his insurance policy. He fled to Canada and lived there for many years, periodically communicating with his wife back in Munising There is nothing more in that grave than a bag of sand."

I now decided that I needed to reconstruct the events of 1908 as closely as I could, drawing on information from newspapers, U.S. government archives, interviews, and the records of the Cleveland Cliffs Iron Company, which had purchased Grand Island in 1900. I found that different people looked at the events of 1908 with very different eyes, each version reflecting specific prejudices and interests. But here is what we know:

On June 3, 1908, George Genry (aka Genery) the veteran 15-year keeper of North Light on Grand Island in Lake Superior, left the lighthouse by sailboat to go to the town of Munising for supplies.

George Genry sailing his boat, early 1900's. Courtesy of Alger County Historical Society

It was approximately a 15-mile over-water trip in a sailboat without a motor along a deserted coast. He left the assistant keeper, Edward C. Morrison, who had taken his position only 6 weeks before, in charge of the light. Genry assigned Morrison a demanding task, since he would have to stay up all night for several days to tend the light; in the keeper's absence there was no possibility for the keeper and assistant keeper to alternate four-hour watches.

Genry picked up supplies in Munising and visited for several days with family members, who resided in the town in a house that still stands.

415 Superior Street. Photo by Loren Graham.

He told his wife, Johanna (Shea) Genry, that in a week, after school let out, he would return to Munising to get her and their children to return to the lighthouse for the summer

The *Marquette Mining Journal* reported on June 22, 1908, that Genry "had been drinking in the town, and was pretty well under the influence of liquor when he left," a charge later denied by the Genry family.

Whatever his state of sobriety, between ten and eleven o'clock on the morning of June 6 Genry started in his sailboat back to the lighthouse, going up the east side of the island. As he passed the East Channel Light (South Light) on the south side of the island (an abandoned lighthouse today, much photographed by tourists on Pictured Rocks Cruise Boats) the keeper of the light, his friend Timothy Dee, waved to him. As he continued on past the entrance to Trout Bay he was seen by another friend, Levi Brown, a commercial fisherman whose family has left its name in Munising for "Brown's Addition," where commercial fishermen still operate today. Brown was evidently the last person to see Genry before his disappearance.

After this sighting, silence set in.

Then, as already related, six days later, on June 12, the boat with the body in it was found by the two hunters near Seven Mile Creek, about 20 miles east of Munising, Their report of their find led to the report of the jury in Grand Marais that the unknown man had died of exposure and injuries unknown to all here.

Keeper Irvine's opinion that the boat was from North Light, Grand Island, and that the body was that of the assistant keeper E. S. Morrison was soon substantiated by J. J. Murray, game keeper for William Mathers' wildlife preserve on Grand Island.

On June 17 a newspaper in Flint Michigan headlined a story "Keeper's Wife Not Worried; Believed She Knows the Location of Missing Genery." The article reported that Genry's wife "is not exercised over his disappearance and it is believed that she is withholding information." Furthermore, the Flint paper recorded, "Genery's wife said he and Morrison quarreled often." There was great disagreement in the newspaper accounts over whether the body showed signs of violence. *The Washington Post, New York Times,* and the *Chicago Tribune* all reported great violence to the body, but the *Munising News* reported on June 19 "His face and head were slightly bruised but no bones were broken. His face had turned black when the body was found but there were no marks of violence." This report seemed to ignore the reports of a broken arm given by both Captain Truedell and the coroner's jury.

The coroner's report saying that the man had died of exposure and injuries of unknown cause was denounced by many people—including persons who later gave differing accounts of what must have happened; a second coroner's report was called for. The opinion issued in this second coroner's report is sharply disputed in newspaper accounts. According to an article in the *Flint Daily Journal*, the members of the jury "were not able to tell how the young man came to his death, but that there was a strong suspicion of murder." However, the official recording of the second coroner's report was "death from exposure," a verdict that was later questioned both by the Morrison and Genry families, but for strikingly different reasons. They both claimed that the coroner was bought off by people who did not want the truth out, but they had different views of what the truth was.

Munising, Grand Marais, Flint (the home of Morrison), and Marquette were now swept with rumors. On June 17 the wife of Morrison reported to Flint newspapers that she had just received a letter from her dead husband in which he reported he feared violence at Genry's hand.

A photo of Lena and Edward Morrison. Photo courtesy of Jo Lee Dibert-Fitko, great-niece of Edward Morrison.

On June 19 the *Port Austin News* reported that "Suspicion is strong that Morrison was murdered by Genery (sic) and cast adrift in the sail boat." However, the same day the *Munising News* published an article saying it is thought Genery (sic) and his assistant went out in the sailboat about two miles from Grand Island to get some fish out of a net. It is almost certain neither man had on a coat when he started on the trip. An empty pint bottle, which Genery had filled with whiskey before he left Munising, was found near the North Light landing on the island. The supposition is that Genery fell out of the boat and was drowned, that his assistant, being unable to steer the craft to land, died from hunger and exposure on Lake Superior.

This *Munising News* story seems to have enraged everybody.

Mrs. Genry claimed that her husband never drank to excess and said the pint whiskey bottle found near the boat landing after her husband's disappearance proves nothing as it was "no uncommon thing for whiskey bottles thrown into Lake Superior to be cast upon the shore at the North Light landing." F. G. Menke of Detroit, who was a good friend of Morrison, was outraged at the suggestion that Morrison, after Genry fell out of the boat, would have been unable to handle a small sailboat. Menke asserted in an article published in the *Detroit Free Press*, "Morrison was an able seaman and perfectly familiar with boats of all kinds. Morrison was the owner of a 32-foot sailboat on the Detroit River, and he had given repeated evidence of his skill in handling the craft under all sorts of conditions." Days passed and then a month. Morrison's body was shipped by train to Flint, Michigan, and buried there in Avondale Cemetery.

No news of Genry appeared. On June 25, nineteen days after she said she had last seen her husband, Mrs. George Genry went to the local newspaper office, the Munising News, to complain of her destitute situation. She said that her husband had been paid some weeks ago, but had disappeared before giving her any money. She had five children to care for, the oldest 13, the youngest six months, and she had no money to buy them food. She said that the family had never been able to save any money because of the meager salary a lighthouse keeper received, and they had been dependent on food from Grand Island supplied by her husband, which included game, fish, and berries. Now that source of food was gone. She asserted that her husband had a life insurance policy for several thousand dollars with an insurance company called "The Modern Woodmen," (the company still exists today) but the firm would not pay until his death had been proven. She appealed for help to the newspaper, which responded with an article in which it stated "The case of this poor woman and her helpless little ones should excite the sympathy and command the help of every citizen in Munising whenever she needs it." Evidently some money was collected.

Then on Friday, July 17, the *Munising News* announced that the previous Saturday, July 11, R. C. Mackenzie and Ben Cook discovered a body near Beaver

THE LAUNCH "LYLE D" MUNISING,MICH.

The boat "Lyle D" which allegedly brought George Genry's body back to Munising on July 17, 1908. Reproduced with permission of Superior View Studio

Beach on Lake Superior, a roadless remote spot, about 20 miles from Munising. The body had been cast far up the beach by the waves and, in the opinion of the coroner, Dr. Theodore Scholtes of Munising, had lain on the beach four or five days when found. The body was considerably decomposed but was identified as that of Genry by clothing and "certain papers" found upon it. The launch Lyle D. of Munising was sent out to bring back the body to the city Saturday evening. Reports on the condition of the body and the means of identification of it are far skimpier in the case of Genry than of Morrison. Because of the decomposition of the corpse the family said that it was quickly buried in the local cemetery.

Soon thereafter, according to the newspaper, the insurance company Modern Woodmen paid Mrs. Genry $2000, a sum that may seem small today but was more than three times the lightkeeper's annual salary.

CHAPTER VII

MUNISING AND THE ESTABLISHMENT

unising in 1908 was a blue-collar town that harbored deep suspicions of any outside establishment, whether it be the wealthy capitalists with their logging and mining companies centered in Marquette and Calumet or governmental authorities. There was a deep belief that the "authorities" always get things wrong. Furthermore, the town was home to ethnic prejudices, not only about the relationship between whites and Native Americans, but also about other ethnic groups. Munising was a town that fitted the historian Robert Wiebe's description of late-nineteenth century America as a collection of "island communities" in which local values reigned.[1]

Many people in Munising disliked George Genry. He was described as extremely authoritarian, surly in his attitudes to others, a heavy drinker, and a frequent brawler. Furthermore, he was part Indian. Genry was extremely sensitive to criticism, and if anyone openly referred to him as a "half-breed," as people often did behind his back, a fight was on.

Many people in town knew that Genry brooked no criticism or opposition, and many knew that he had great difficulty keeping an assistant keeper at the lighthouse. During the fifteen years that Genry was keeper of Old North Light there were 12 different assistant keepers, indicating that Genry had great trouble getting anybody to work with him. He assigned his assistants all the dirty jobs, and often asked them to take care of the light while he went into town for drunken bouts. The assistant was expected to stay up all night for several nights tending the light. Yet during the day Genry required him to keep the station in immaculate condition.

One of Genry's assistant keepers, William C. Marshall, found Genry so difficult to get along with that in 1905 he simply ran away from the lighthouse and completely disappeared, perhaps ending up in one of the

---

1   Robert Wiebe, op. cit.

anonymous lumber camps. The Lighthouse Board in Washington, D.C. fired Marshall for "abandoning his post" and appointed Albert J. Smith in his place. Smith lasted all of two months, when he also quit. The next two assistant keepers, Joseph Metivier and Edward Sommer, lasted one season each.

After Genry's disappearance in 1908 investigators in the lighthouse found a packet of letters of complaint against him, accompanied in each case by Genry's denial of all charges; Genry castigated his assistant keepers as lazy miscreants.

Genry had ample opportunity to try to refute criticism of him forwarded to Washington. The "Instructions to Light-Keepers" issued by the Light House Board to all light stations laid down strict rules by which complaints could be made by assistant keepers against their superior keeper. The rules read as follows:

> When a keeper neglects his duties it is the imperative duty of each assistant at the station to report the facts without delay, in writing, to the inspector. The reported keeper must be furnished with a copy of the complaints made against him, at least three days before such complaints are forwarded, so that he may, if he sees fit, transmit a statement to the inspector with the report.

Genry must have had a friend or two on the Lighthouse Board because he was never officially reprimanded. Seven of the nine members of that board were U.S. Army or U.S. Navy officers, assigned temporary duty with the Light-House Establishment before returning to their military or naval assignments. These men appreciated the need for authority in a government organization like the Light House Establishment.

Notice that the above rules cite only "neglect of duties" as reason for valid complaint against a keeper. Having a disagreeable personality or being authoritarian was not enough to justify a complaint. In fact, being authoritarian was even sanctioned by the rules, which stated that assistants "are required to observe the orders of the keepers in all matters connected with the duties of the Light-House Establishment. Any disobedience of such orders will be held as a sufficient cause for recommending the discharge of the assistant."

Even abuse of alcohol was difficult to prove as reason for criticism of a keeper, since the rules stated that intoxication "while on duty" was the reason for suspension. Genry was careful to assign the assistant keeper as the person on watch at the light when he left the station to go to town for his alcoholic bouts.

On August 30, 1901, the Naval Secretary of the Light-House Board in Washington wrote Keeper Genry a letter noting "The Board is gratified to learn that the station under your charge is in excellent condition. The Board is glad to commend you for attention to duty and efficiency in performing it, and will note this fact on its records and have it to be entered on the books in the office of the Inspector, as a part of your official history." Several weeks later, Genry's assistant keeper at the time, Robert Allen, quit his job expressing dissatisfaction with the conditions of his employment. Genry invariably gave him the most difficult tasks and inconvenient watches.

On May 1, 1908, Keeper Genry was assigned a new assistant keeper, Edward Morrison, to replace Edward Sommer. Morrison had many qualities that made conflict with Genry seem likely. He had served in the U.S. Navy in China and the Philippines, and he believed that he understood boats and maritime matters better than Genry did. (The lighthouse authorities preferred ex-sailors as employees, since seamen were accustomed to standing watches at night and understood the problems of ships at sea.) Morrison was contemptuous of Genry's inability to swim. He also took great pride in the fact that he was a "white American" and sometimes referred to Genry in letters home as a "whiskey-drinking Half Breed." Morrison is depicted below in a photo taken in Japan, probably around 1900:

Photo by "K. Kagasaki, Yokohama, Japan. Photo courtesy of Jo Lee Dibert-Fitko and Hiawatha National Forest

When Morrison received his new appointment he came to Munising and befriended a number of people in town and on Grand Island, including J. J. Murray, William Mather's game keeper on Grand Island. Murray told Morrison that Genry was a poacher who encouraged other Indians to kill Mather's prize game. The next time Murray would see Morrison was when he identified his body.

We do not know when disagreements arose between Genry and Morrison, but it must have been within days of their beginning to work together. Genry forced Morrison to live in the basement and strictly controlled all his contacts with the outside world. Morrison's salary and all his mail went through Genry's hands before reaching him (we have a postcard from Morrison's brother in Flint mailed to him on May 22, 1908; it is addressed simply: "Mr. E. S. Morrison, c/o George Genry, Munising, Michigan") According to the Morrison family, Edward Morrison wrote home to his wife in Flint, Michigan, in early June, 1908, "Do not be surprised if you hear of my body being found dead along the shore of Lake Superior." He continued that Keeper Genry was of a "quarrelsome disposition" and said he feared an assault if he opposed him. Mrs. Morrison did not receive the letter until after she had already been informed of her husband's disappearance.

It is not surprising, therefore, that Murray and many other people in Munising assumed that Genry had murdered Morrison in a brawl. Noting that when Morrison's body was found in the boat there was a hole in the hull, approximately four by one inches and a small ax, they advanced the following speculation: After killing Morrison, Genry got in another of the lighthouse boats in the boat house (there were three boats) and rowed out into the bay, towing the boat with Morrison's body behind him. At a suitable distance, Genry allegedly chopped a small hole in Morrison's boat with a hatchet, and then left the boat with Morrison's body to go adrift, slowly taking on water. The town speculators then assumed that Genry took a boat into town, informed his wife what had happened, and, several days later fled to Canada, where he went into hiding but remained in periodic communication with his wife.

When this speculation circulated in Munising, rumors went wild. Some people swore that they "knew" other people who had seen Genry drinking in Munising on June 9 and 10, several days after he had originally departed for the lighthouse on June 6 If this were true, it would prove that Genry did not share Morrison's fate in the lake.

After the disappearance of Keeper George Genry in June, 1908, the Lighthouse Board appointed Commander James T. Smith, United States Navy, to investigate the incident. Commander Smith was the Inspector of the 11th District, U. S. Light House Establishment, based in Detroit, and had served in that position since September 30, 1906. Smith had met Genry several times during his inspection trips on Lake Superior aboard the steamer *Amaranth*. He had never met Morrison. But the previous year, 1907, Smith had descended upon North Light in a surprise inspection trip and found it in perfect order.

Commander Smith came to Munising in July, 1908, and talked to local people, many of whom tried to convince him that this was a story of a murder, a dastardly act, a case in which the lighthouse keeper George Genry murdered the assistant keeper Edward Morrison. Smith found in Munising considerable animosity toward Genry and sympathy with the dead assistant keeper, Morrison. And the town residents relished a lurid story of murder, just as the newspapers did.

But when Commander Smith tried to nail down facts that would point to Genry as the murderer, he came up empty. For example, he was told in Munising that people had seen Genry drinking in Munising on June 9 and 10, "proving" that he survived the incident. When Smith asked for the identities of these witnesses, no names were produced. Many people had "heard" the story that Genry returned to Munising, but no actual witnesses could be found, although Smith made the rounds of all the local saloons and asked for help from the town citizens. Smith could not find a single person who had actually seen Genry on June 9 and 10, as alleged.

Another weakness in the story being told in Munising that Smith soon found concerned the lighthouse boats. According to the people who accused Genry of murder, after killing Morrison he returned from the lighthouse to the town of Munising, a twelve-mile boat trip. That would mean, observed Smith, that one of the three boats at the lighthouse boat house should be missing. But when Smith went to the boat house, he found two of the boats safely in place, and the third was the one that Morrison's body was found in. Genry, therefore, could not have returned to town in one of the lighthouse boats, as alleged.

On July 9, 1908, Commander Smith submitted a report to the Light House Board in Washington DC in which he determined that both men died of accidental causes. According to Smith, after the two men had unloaded the supplies that Genry brought from Munising they decided to go out in a boat to get some dinner fish from the fish nets that they had placed near the island. While they were out in the lake Smith surmised that they were hit by a sudden squall, or, possibly, the boat overturned in the process of raising the nets. The boat was dismasted, the oars and rudder were swept away. Genry could not swim and was surely drowned. Commander Smith thought that Morrison, an experienced swimmer, managed to get the boat righted, and crawled in. Without oars or a rudder he could not control the boat. He drifted around on the lake for days, died of exposure, and then his body rolled back and forth in the boat, giving his head the injuries that were earlier described as blows that killed him and disfigured his face. Commander Smith concluded, "the suspicion of foul play is not well founded."

The government's report was widely dismissed by Munising people who knew both Genry and Morrison. (Many more knew Genry than Morrison, since the assistant keeper had just arrived in Munising earlier in the summer, while Genry and his family had lived in the area for many years.) The critics of the government verdict protested that the Navy officer refused to pay attention to reports of enmity between the two men and ignored the possibility that Genry had fled the scene, but was still in secret communication with his family. They asked why Mrs. Genry seemed so little disturbed by her husband's disappearance. They also said that Commander Smith was too willing to accept the views of Timothy Dee, keeper of South Light and a defender of Genry's reputation. They suspected Dee, a government employee and fellow Chippewa, of supplying an alibi for Genry. And they dismissed the government report on the incident supplied by Commander Smith. One of the arguments they used against it was that although Smith surmised a "sudden squall" overturned the boat, locals reported good weather on June 6. They ignored Smith's observation in his report that the boat could have overturned in the process of the two men leaning over the same side and raising the nets.

Commander Smith issued his report on July 9, before Genry's body was reported found on July 11. A day later a funeral was held for Genry and he was allegedly buried in Maple Grove cemetery. Commander Smith felt vindicated.

But the rumors in town could not be silenced. According to some townspeople the alleged discovery of a body near Beaver Beach identified as George Genry was falsified so that Mrs. Genry could claim the $2000 insurance policy from the Modern Woodmen insurance company. According to these people she had the help of sympathizers in Munising, including the coroner, Dr. Theodore Scholtes, who were convinced that Genry was dead, but that his body would never be found, since, as the old saying went, "Lake Superior Never Gives Up its Dead." The water in the lake was so cold that submerged bodies allegedly do not putrefy and rise to the surface, but instead remain submerged on the bottom of the lake indefinitely. According to this version, the reason Morrison's body was found was that it was in a boat on the surface; Genry's, on the other hand, had supposedly sunk to the bottom of Lake Superior.

Furthermore, T. L. Morrison of Flint, Michigan, the brother of the dead assistant keeper, wrote on July 21, 1908, a letter to the Light House Board in Washington, D.C., disputing Commander Smith's report, and claiming that contrary to the assertions of Genry's friend Timothy Dee, Genry's body was never found. Morrison alleged that the finding of the body had been fabricated in order to provide cover for the fugitive Genry and justification for the payment of his insurance policy. The brother of the assistant keeper further asserted "Genry is still alive and his friend up there inserted the account (of his death – LRG)." The brother continued, "I will also suggest that Mrs. Genery (sic) didn't fear for her husband's safety at the time Morrison was found. It would then appear that she knows where he is." The brother said he had heard that Genry was in the "Canadian Northwest." T. L. Morrison further asserted that his brother was "a sober American (White) and should have some preference over a Whiskey drinking Half breed, as I understand Genery was." He signed his letter of protest "T. L. Morrison (A White American)"

Although the government account issued by Commander Smith is the official verdict of the incident valid to the present day, it was never accepted by many members of the Munising community, as illustrated by Bill Cox's conversation with me 67 years later.

And I found out in 1980, several years later, from yet another Munising resident that the suspicion of Genry had not died in the community memory. This event was connected with our Servel propane refrigerator at the lighthouse, an ancient device we needed to keep working since, without electricity, we could not use an electric refrigerator. We needed a refrigerator that ran on propane gas, no longer available in local stores. Unfortunately, one summer our propane refrigerator stopped working and refused to respond to any of my normal remedies, which included "burping" it by moving it back and forward in a motion intended to get air bubbles out of the propane.

I needed to find someone who knew how to repair propane refrigerators, not an easy task in the nearby small town of Munising, population about 3000. Inquiring at a local hardware store I learned from my good friend Peter Benzing that a man named Al Moros supposedly knew how to work on propane refrigerators. I went to visit him at his house on Varnum Street and asked if he would be willing to look at my refrigerator if I took him to the lighthouse by boat and jeep.

He said he would be happy to come to the lighthouse, but asked if it would be all right if his wife Anne came also, since she would enjoy seeing the lighthouse. I readily agreed, and a few days later took both of them to the troublesome refrigerator on the north end of the island.

Al Moros turned out to be quite skilled in looking at propane refrigerators, and soon was taking the thing apart. While he worked in the kitchen his wife Anne sat at the dining table and looked through the materials on the history of the lighthouse that I had been collecting. She discovered a February 21, 1951, letter from Ed Genry to the U.S. Coast Guard asking for a pension for his mother, Johanna Shea Genry. It seems that 43 years after the disappearance of her husband George, Johanna was still living in Munising and had never received from the US government any benefits as a lighthouse keeper's widow. In 1951 Ed Genry wrote in the letter that Anne Moros excitedly held in her hand that his mother would like to apply for a "Widow's Lighthouse Service Annuity."

When Anne Moros saw this letter she cried out, "Why did they wait 43 years to apply for a pension?" Then she answered her own question: "I think I know. Let me tell you a story."

It seems that Johanna (the younger) Genry, a daughter of George and Johanna Shea Genry, had been Anne Moros' elementary school teacher

James T. Smith, who investigated the events at Old North Lighthouse in July, 1908, and concluded that no foul play was involved. Photo taken in 1865, when he was a midshipman at the U.S. Naval Academy. Photo courtesy of U.S. Naval Academy.

in Munising in 1951. Anne recalled that suddenly in 1951 her teacher, Miss Genry, disappeared for a few days to make a trip. Anne remembered the event vividly, because she had been given a substitute teacher for a few days whom she remembered well. Anne then added, "This story fits with what everybody in town believed, that George Genry killed Morrison, fled to Canada, where he lived until his death in 1951. The reason that my teacher Johanna had to suddenly go away was that she went with her mother to George's funeral in Canada. George had finally died. The Genrys were afraid to raise the issue of a pension for George's wife Johanna until George was actually dead. They feared that if they raised it earlier the U.S. government would open the case again and discover that George was still alive. And then it would become clear that George was the murderer in 1908 and fled."

This observation seemed weighty. Just why would Johanna Shea Genery wait until 1951 to apply for a widow's pension if her husband actually died in 1908 and was buried in the local cemetery? Combined with Anne Moros's story about how her teacher, the younger Johanna, disappeared for a few days to Canada in 1951, the finger did seem to point to something strange. All of a sudden I wanted to go to the Munising cemetery and dig down to see if George's casket there was filled, not with a body, but with a bag of sand, as Bill Cox had told me was the case in 1975. Was there a great conspiracy of the Genry family involved here?

I now found myself in the same position that Commander James Smith, USN, was in when he came to Munising in 1908 to investigate the incident. Smith was told by Munising residents that Genry had killed Morrison in the lighthouse, returned for a few days to the town of Munising, and then fled to Canada. Smith probed the story and could find no witnesses to Genry's return, even though people said "many people saw Genry in the local saloons." Under investigation the rumors were found to be baseless. Now I needed to probe another local story to see if it stood up.

The first thing I did was to investigate more fully the circumstances of the 1951 application by the Genry family to the Coast Guard for a widow's pension for Johanna Shea Genry. I knew that in 1908 U.S. lighthouses were not administered by the Coast Guard, but the Commerce Department. Did the Coast Guard automatically assume all past obligations of the Commerce Department, including widow's pensions for keepers who died before 1939, when the Coast Guard took over lighthouses? I began looking into the legislation on the social benefits of lighthouse keepers and their families.

I soon discovered something that was the equivalent of Commander Smith's inability to find a witness to George Genry's alleged return to Munising after "murdering" Morrison. It turns out that not until August 19, 1950, did the U.S. government pass legislation that provided for "Benefits for surviving spouses of Lighthouse Service employees."[2] Before that time Johanna Shea Genry was not eligible for a widow's pension. In fact, even keepers themselves had no pensions in 1908 (they came in 1918 but did not provide for widows).[3] Ed Genry, the son of George, was a U.S. postmaster, and he no doubt kept track of legislation on social benefits of government employees. He discovered that on August 19, 1950, the government had passed a law covering people like his mother. We know that Ed was aware of this law because in one of his letters to the Coast Guard he cited the "Act of August 19, 1950" on "Widow's Lighthouse Service Annuities." So Ed Genry applied for a pension for his mother just seven months after such pensions became available for the first time. Anne Moros's accusatory question "Why did she wait 43 years before applying for a pension?" had a very logical answer.

---

2   33 USC 772, August 19, 1950, ch. 761, Sec. 1, 64 Stat. 465.
3   "Great Lakes Lighthouses," Center for U.P. Studies, Northern Michigan University, http://wbb.nmu.edu/Centers/Upper Peninsula Studies/SiteSections/UPHistory/FolkloreHistory/ Lighthouses.shtm, accessed on December 1, 2009.

CHAPTER VIII

INDIAN HUNTING RIGHTS AND ACCUSATIONS OF SKULDUGGERY

The Genry family continued to live in Munising for many years. In fact, at least one person connected to the family, an adopted grand-daughter, lives there still. In 1977 I invited Johanna Genry (the younger), a daughter of George Genry, to return to the lighthouse for the first time since 1907. For many years she had been a school teacher in Munising, but now she was retired. All her life she lived in Munising in the house where she was born, the original home of George and Johanna Shea Genry. She came to the lighthouse with Isabella Sullivan, the president of the Alger County Historical Society. The picture below shows Johanna sitting between Isabella and my wife at the dining table of the recently-restored Old North Lighthouse.

Photo by Loren Graham

On this occasion I inquired into the details of the 1908 disappearance of her father, but Johanna did not want to talk about it. She had been ten years old at the time, and she said she knew what happened, but she refused to elaborate. Her interest was entirely in another matter. She told us that in 1907 William Mather, president of the Cleveland Cliffs Iron Company, had launched a resort hotel on the south end of the island, and that a horse and carriage regularly brought tourists to the lighthouse.

(The roads on the island were evidently in a lot better shape in 1907 than they were in 1977; I had to bring Isabella Sullivan and Johanna Genry to the lighthouse in a four-wheel drive Toyota Landcruiser with a winch and 150 feet of aircraft cable on the front bumper; the winch permitted us to get through the large mud holes in the trail). According to Johanna at the end of the summer of 1907 she had buried at the base of the lighthouse "all her nickels" that came from her refreshment sales. When her father unexpectedly disappeared in June, 1908, Johanna was not able to return that summer to the lighthouse as she had expected, and she had never retrieved her childhood fortune. Now, sixty-nine years later, she wanted to get her nickels.

I got a shovel and asked Johanna to show me where to dig for her nickels. She confidently pointed to a spot near the base of the lighthouse tower and I began to dig. After getting about two feet deep she suddenly said "No, they wouldn't be that deep. You are digging in the wrong place. Dig over here," pointing to a spot several feet from the first one. I immediately began to dig again, only to have the same verdict pronounced on my efforts. After I had dug about five or six holes, and was rapidly becoming exhausted, it became apparent that the 79-year-old Johanna no longer remembered exactly what she had done with her nickels in 1907. We eventually gave up the search for the nickels, and they have never been found to this day.

On October 21, 1981, seventy-three years after the disappearance of George Genry and Edward Morrison from Old North Light, I conducted an hour-long taped interview with two of George Genry's children, Mary Genry Krueger and Ed Genry. Both of them had spent most of their lives in the town of Munising, and the older of them, Mary, had many memories of the lighthouse, where she had lived every summer until she was eleven or twelve years old.

The question which I most wanted to ask them, of course, was "Is it true, as some people in Munising believe, that your father murdered Ed Morrison in 1908 and fled to Canada?" Asking such a question would not be easy, however, since I was a guest in the house of George Genry's daughter, and talking with his son, a prominent and respected person in Munising and its longtime postmaster. I decided, therefore, to approach the question only after a lengthy conversation on other subjects.

I asked them what it was like to live at the lighthouse, where they got water (a question plaguing my wife and me at the time), whether their parents worried about the possibility the children would fall off the cliff while playing, and similar questions. They answered that they enjoyed playing around the lighthouse, often setting up a playhouse table in the yard, that they got water from a well to the southeast of the lighthouse, and that their parents would not allow them to go near the cliffs.

From the very beginning of our talks, facts and observations emerged that had at a least an indirect bearing on the stories I had been hearing. Their father, they said, was born and raised in Ontonagon, a town in the Upper Peninsula of Michigan with a historic Native American population. George Genry's children did not say that their father was of Chippewa descent, but they implied it. One of George Genry's closest friends, they added, was Jimmy Kishketog, the full-blooded Chippewa who lived in Indiantown, near Munising. According to Genry's children, Jimmy Kishketog would often visit at the lighthouse, and George would invite him to live for several days in the nearby toolshed, where he preferred to sleep on the floor, not in a bed. It seems that George Genry and Jimmy Kishketog very much enjoyed talking together. When I asked the children what the two talked about they said that they had been too young to remember. I later learned from the Alger County Centennial History, published a few years later, in 1986, that Jimmy Kishketog lived on until 1930, always adhering to Chippewa traditions, both in religion and in life style. He was an avid and skilled deer hunter and would not observe hunting regulations, considering the wild animals of the forests to be his for the taking, as they always had been for his ancestors in previous centuries. Ed and Mary Genry confessed that their father also often killed deer out of season. Jimmy would sometimes take a saddle of deer (a cut comprising both loins) from the island into town to sell. He would also, at George Genry's suggestion, give meat to the Genry family in Munising. When I then asked Ed and Mary their opinions about the local Native American community, many of whom lived in Indiantown where Kishketog had a cabin, they were somewhat elusive, displaying the reluctance of their generation to betray Indian sympathies or kinship, but Ed Genry did observe that "many of the Indians were actually very nice people."

Jimmy Kishketog. Photo from the collection of Theodore Paquette Sr. and wife Mabel Carr Paquette and family, with help of Dolores LeVeque and Viola Paquette Magnuson.

Ed Genry and Mary Genry Krueger also told me their mother, Johanna Shea, was an Irishwoman related to the Malone family, and that many members of this family worked for the U.S. Lighthouse Establishment. Their father had gotten his first position in the lighthouse service through his wife's sister's husband, who was at that time the head keeper of Rock of Ages Light, another remote Lake Superior station. There were nine Malone brothers and all of them, or almost all of them, worked as lighthouse keepers or as crewmen on lighthouse tenders, including the Amaranth, which serviced and inspected Lake Superior lights. The Malones knew how to curry favor with officials in the Lighthouse Service. They named eleven of their children in honor of the sitting district inspector.[1] Such close connections between George Genry and other people in the lighthouse service might explain why all the complaints about Genry forwarded on to the Lighthouse Board by the unhappy assistant keepers failed to result in a reprimand. It might also help explain why George's lighthouse always got high marks from the allegedly "surprise" inspection visits of the steamer Amaranth. George had relatives on board who could tell him of the likely times the inspection would occur, and he also had many supporters in the lighthouse workforce.

But one of the biggest surprises that emerged in the early, socially comfortable part of the conversation, was their description of their father. "George Genry was," according to his daughter, "a good-natured man, the sort of person who got on with everyone. He was not the fighting kind." This observation contradicted many previous stories, some of them published in local newspapers, about the difficult, hot-tempered lighthouse keeper. Once again, the stories about the 1908 events contradicted each other.

After over a half-hour of chatting with the Genry children (Mary was 84, Ed was 74) I finally managed to work my way toward the question I wished to ask. Putting everything in a conditional, subjunctive mood, I inquired "You know, some people in Munising maintain that your father did not die in 1908. They say that he murdered Morrison and then fled to Canada. Have you ever heard that theory?" Both Genry children asserted

---

1 Patricia Majher, *Ladies of the Lights: Michigan Women in the U.S. Lighthouse Service,* University of Michigan Press, Ann Arbor, 2010, p. 41.

that they had never heard such a story, that it was entirely new to them (something extremely difficult for me to believe, since I had read this version in numerous newspaper articles and heard it from a number of people still alive in Munising in 1981). They said the allegation that their father had murdered Morrison was ridiculous. Not objecting, I replied, "Then this means, evidently, that you accept the U.S. government report maintaining that their deaths were accidental, and that no foul play was involved?"

To my amazement, Ed Genry quickly replied, "Oh no, the government version is even more preposterous. It was definitely a case of murder."

"Well then," I interjected, "who murdered whom? Do you think that Morrison murdered your father?"

At this point a whole different version of the events of 1908 emerged, one that I had never heard before. This interpretation was embedded in the history of Grand Island in the first decade of the last century, and the Genry family's reaction to recent changes to the island. As related earlier, in 1900 the Cleveland Cliffs Iron Company purchased Grand Island—all of it except for two pieces of land that belonged to the U.S. government for the purposes of lighthouses: Old North Light at the north end of the island, and "East Channel Light," often called "South Light" at the south end of the island. The iron company was not interested in mining on the island— there was no iron ore there—but in converting it into a game preserve that could also serve as a playground for the top executives of the company, especially its president, William Gwinn Mather.

The Genry children told me that Mather was very irritated at their father, Jimmy Kishketog, and the other lighthouse keeper on the island, Timothy Dee, because they continued to hunt game on the island after Mather bought it, just as they and other Indians had for many centuries before. Furthermore, Mather, they continued, had the great fear that eventually some of the lighthouse land would be sold to "common people such as saloon keepers" and that he would not be able to fulfill his dream for a totally protected game preserve, or, more accurately, a preserve in which only he and his friends could hunt. The amount of land belonging to the government around the lighthouses was much more than was needed for the lighthouses themselves, in all, several hundred acres; Mather feared that the government would eventually sell off part of it. (This eventually happened to the land at South Light, and that land today is the only land on the island in local, private hands.)

Ed Genry said that in the first years of the century "the Cliff" (the term he used for "Cleveland Cliffs Iron Company") was "always arguing with Dad about deer; they said he was killing the deer. The company wanted Dad out of there." (After Genry's disappearance, the *Marquette Mining Journal*, the newspaper in the nearby city of Marquette where Mather and the Cleveland Cliffs company had extensive holdings, observed that Genry had been "a constant thorn in the side of the company.")

The Genrys admitted that their father kept a gun at the kitchen door of the lighthouse and whenever he or his frequent visitors Jimmy Kishketog or Timothy Dee saw one of Mather's prize animals coming up the lighthouse lane he would shoot it and add it to the kitchen larder. According to the Genrys, Mather ordered his men to try to catch Genry in the act of poaching. Ed Genry maintained that Mather's men made Grand Island "a terrible place for his father." He said "the Cliff's men would break into the lighthouse when Dad wasn't there. They knew when he was absent by seeing that one of the boats down at the beach was gone." The Genry children added that their mother knew who some of the Cleveland Cliffs men were who allegedly persecuted her father and the assistant keeper. They are "all dead" now, they said, but they recalled that the name of one of the men was "Fink" (later investigation revealed that a W. O. Fink had been a section foreman on the local railroad, owned by Mather's company, who also took on spare jobs in the area.) Evidently the company men were looking for venison in the lighthouse as evidence that Genry was poaching their game. However, the Genry children observed that their father was skilled at concealing his activities.

According to Ed Genry, telling stories he had heard from his mother, the Cliffs men broke in to the lighthouse several times when his father was gone, ransacking the place; once, Ed said, the Cliffs men intruded into the building only to discover there the assistant keeper (which of the many assistants over the years was not clear), whom they tied to a chair while they searched the house. Ed Genry described the visitations of the Cliffs men to the lighthouse as barbarous acts, the descending upon his father of terrorizing ruffians. The newspaper *Marquette Mining Journal* described those same events in a very different way; Genry, it reported:

> had no sympathy with the company's plan for making Grand Island a game preserve and was a persistent poacher of its domains, keeping the lighthouse larder well supplied with fresh venison and other game. On occasions the light was descended on, by virtue of a search warrant, and an effort made to get evidence sufficient to convict Genery, but he was clever at hiding his game, and escaped arrest. When the light was visited after the tragedy, however, both fresh and salted venison was found.

Alerted by the Genrys, I searched the written records of 1900-1908 and found that William Mather and his assistants at the Cleveland Cliffs Iron Company went to great lengths to try to stop the poaching activities of George Genry. On September 7, 1903, Richard E. Follett of the Land Department of Mather's company wrote to Dr. T. S. Palmer, in charge of Game Preservation of the Department of Agriculture in Washington DC complaining that Mather's prize game animals were being poached on the government sections of the island "where the light houses are located," and asked the government to take action to stop this activity. Evidently nothing was done, or at least nothing that satisfied Mather. (Notice the plural "light houses," implicating George's friend Timothy Dee at South Light in similar poaching.)

More than a year later, on December 2, 1904, Mather proposed to place a fence around the government land. The reason he gave in a letter of that date to the lighthouse authorities was disingenuous, since Mather said he wished to fence off the government land "in order that your keeper and his family may be protected from the game." Mather's goal was not the protection of the keeper's family from the game, but the game from George Genry, Jimmy Kishketog, and Timothy Dee.

The nature of this "game fence" on Grand Island had always bothered me. According to stories told to me by Cleveland Cliffs officials, the fence was supposed to keep Mather's animals from falling off the cliffs or escaping from the island. This rationale made no sense to me, since there were many places on the south end of the island—for example, at Trout

Bay—where the game could even more easily escape, but there was no fence there. But when I learned that the real purpose of the fence was to keep the animals away from George Genry and his guns at the north end, I understood the motivation for putting up the fence. Today, over a hundred years after the fence was erected around the lighthouse land, some of it still remains, while most of it has been leveled by falling trees. Shown below is a remnant of the fence; notice how the tree has grown around it in the decades since it was installed, so that now the wires are almost half-way into the tree:

Photo by Loren Graham

The fence failed to achieve its purpose. It had gates in it for the passage of the lighthouse personnel down to the beach, and the keepers frequently left the gates open so that the game could approach the lighthouse. Furthermore, poaching evidently continued at such a rate that Mather and his men suspected that when no one was around, Genry, Kishketog, and Dee had no compunctions about hunting on the land that belonged to Mather, the land on the other side of the fence. In a word, the fence meant nothing to Genry and his hunting friends.

In the interview with the Genry children in 1981 Ed Genry said that after several unsuccessful years of trying to get Genry removed from his post Mather told his men "Get Genry, but don't tell me how you did it." When I queried Ed Genry if he was certain that Mather himself gave this order, he replied, "Either he gave it or he made so clear to his men what he wanted that it was the same as an order." Genry was certain that his father was murdered by men from the Cleveland Cliffs Iron Company.

According to the Genry children, the likely scenario was as follows. George Genry had been in Munising, leaving Ed Morrison, the assistant keeper, in charge of the lighthouse. Morrison was preparing dinner for both of them; later, after their disappearance, they said the prepared dinner was found in the lighthouse. Morrison evidently looked out the window on the east side of the lighthouse and saw Genry approaching the beach below in the lighthouse boat. (The Genry account here differs from some others that placed Morrison in the tool shed when Genry's boat appeared; the window to which the Genrys referred is today in my wife's study, and affords a good view of the eastern approach to the lighthouse

Morrison then got a wheelbarrow and went down to the beach to help unload the supplies. The two men hung their coats on the hooks in the

Photo by Loren Graham

boathouse and got to work. While they were unloading the supplies and putting them in the boathouse a group of Cleveland Cliffs men came upon them. An argument immediately broke out, since the Cliffs men were on lighthouse land, not land belonging to the company, and Genry permitted people on "his" land only with his permission. The argument became more and more strained, with accusations of poaching no doubt quickly surfacing, and eventually the Cliffs men killed both Genry and Morrison, or, as Ed Genry later described it, "dipped them off." The company men had not intended to kill the assistant keeper, but since he was there as a witness, he was also dispatched. Then the Cliffs men put Morrison's body in the boat and pushed it out into the lake, hoping his death would be considered accidental. They must have hidden Genry's body at this moment. According to the Genry children, the body was later produced by the same men who killed the lighthouse keeper.

Ed Genry continued that almost a month after the murder the local physician in town, who also served as coroner, Dr. Theodore Scholtes, approached his mother and told her that Cleveland Cliffs men on the island were looking along the shore for her husband's body (on the alleged assumption that he had died accidentally in the lake along with Morrison) but that "they would look harder if she posted a reward for the body." Ed and Mary Genry surmised that these men had the body all along, but were just looking for a way to make some money in delivering it up. According to the Genrys, their mother replied, "No, I cannot afford to. I have five kids I have to raise." Dr. Scholtes then allegedly said "They already have the body, but don't want to give it up unless you pay money." She refused.

A few days later, the Genry children continued, Ed Vendien, who had a local garage in Munising, found George's body on Chapel Beach, 13 miles from Munising; (The Genry account here differs from the report in the *Munising News* on July 17, 1908, that said the men who found the body were R.C. Mackenzie and Ben Cook) . According to the Genry children, by this time the body had so decomposed that the signs of foul play were no longer visible.

The Genrys continued that after the body was found an attorney from Grand Marais, a neighboring town, approached Mrs. Genry and said "I would like to take up this case against the Cleveland Cliffs Iron Company. There definitely is foul play involved here. I will do it for nothing if necessary, but the Genrys could become rich people out of the judgment that I think I can get."

Ed Genry continued that his mother would not let the attorney take up the case. "She was scared. The Cliff's guys did what they wanted. They owned everything—the judges, the police, the coroners. If you went to court, you might as well forget it. And once you took action against the company, it would never forgive you. My mother had five children and one of them might want to work for the company some day, since it was the largest employer in the area. They would never hire a Genry if they were known to be opponents of the company."

Fascinated by this conversation, I asked, if it was the case that both Genry and Morrison had been killed, would not a skilled physician be able, in an autopsy, to determine the cause of death even after some decomposition. Ed Genry replied, "Nobody would testify against the Cliff. They were powerful. Still are. And there was no such thing as a good autopsy in this area in those days." The alleged coroners' reports, he said, were frauds, since the coroners were owned by "the Cliff." And he added, "The story that my father killed Morrison was put out by the Cliff as a cover story." (I noted to myself that earlier Ed Genry had said that he had never before heard the story that his father was the murderer; now he seemed to be admitting that he knew about it, and attributed it to the company.)

The Genrys went on to tell a rather detailed story supporting the view that their father died in June, 1908. Mary Genry Krueger said that the undertaker asked her mother to come to the funeral home to identify the body. Mary said that she accompanied her mother to the funeral home but indicated that she was not with her mother when the undertaker pulled back the sheet over the decomposed body. But Mary described her mother's reaction as "That's him." Mary continued that her mother actually seemed relieved, for now she would be able to collect on the insurance policy.

Neither of the surviving Genry children expressed any interest, after 73 years, in returning to the lighthouse (although their sister Johanna, now deceased, had been eager to do so several years earlier to look for her nickels). Ed observed that it was still "a terrible place."

In the nineteen fifties and sixties the sole permanent resident of Grand Island was Harry Powell, a descendant of one of the pioneer families of Alger County. Harry lived alone on the island in the winters, surviving in a house that was so filled with junk that anything taken into it and put down was lost forever. In 1970 his island house burned to the ground, and he moved over to the mainland to Powell's Point, where he was born. His departure left Grand Island without any year-round residents for the first time in hundreds of years. Shortly before Harry's death in 1982 he came back for a visit to the island, brought over by Tony Beich, one of the summer people from the island. I met Harry again at that time and mentioned to him my interest in the events surrounding Genry's disappearance; did he know anything about it? Of course he remembered the event, he said. He had been 12 years old at the time, and everybody talked about the incident for days. He said his father Curran Powell often worked on the island for Cleveland Cliffs and knew Genry. Shortly before Curran's death Harry said that his father told him, "I know what happened to George Genry and Ed Morrison, but I will never tell." Was the Genry family story that George was killed by men working for Cleveland Cliffs true, and was Curran Powell one of those men?

Despite the many fascinating details the Genrys gave, their story troubled me. The only persons I have ever heard this version from are Genrys, whose motives might be suspected, since their story exculpates the family. True, the remark from Harry Powell about how his father knew what happened but would never tell points to a secret crime. Curran Powell would never have said that if he thought that the government version was correct, that Genry died of natural causes in June 1908. But if the Genrys were merely making excuses, and George actually killed Ed Morrison, it was still possible that the Powells would conceal the story, since the Powells and the Genrys were both local island families and knew each other. They were also both part Native American and probably felt some common bonds.

But several things that the Genry children told me shed light on these longago events. Part of the conflict in this story was between Native Americans who considered the wild game in the forest to be theirs for the taking, and new white authorities who were moving in, both the state game wardens and the officials of the Cleveland Cliffs Iron Company. These new outsiders thought they had the right to regulate the taking of game and punish people who did not follow the new rules. Game laws were still a new phenomenon in the Upper Peninsula in the early years of the twentieth century. It is true that in 1887 Michigan had appointed its first State Game Warden, but the game laws were enforced only in settled areas. Much of the Upper Peninsula was still wilderness, and few people cared about hunting regulations. Certainly the "market hunters" for the lumber camps ignored them. Not until 1895 did Michigan require a license (fifty cents) to hunt deer with a firearm, and this new law was enforced only in places where there were authorities present. When this law was passed George Genry had already been keeper of North Light for two years, and was thoroughly accustomed to killing deer whenever he wished. Living in a spot many miles from the nearest habitation, the law was non-existent so far as he was concerned. It had been that way for all previous keepers, some of them Chippewa like him.

If the new game laws were defied by many whites in wilderness areas, they were often totally ignored, even scorned, by the Native Americans. George Genry, Jimmy Kishketog, and Timothy Dee were all part native – in Kishketog's case, a pureblood. Therefore it was not even clear if the laws applied to them. We have seen that the Treaty of Washington of 1836 gave the Chippewa the right to continue to fish and hunt these lands. Furthermore, the same treaty reserved part of Grand Island for the Chippewa, a provision that William Mather ignored. Jimmy Kishketog aptly observed that "the white men make treaties to get what they want and then they violate their own treaties."

The Treaty of Washington of 1836 stated that Indian rights continued on the lands ceded "until the land is required for settlement."[2] In terms of settlement, Grand Island in the early twentieth century was moving in a direction opposite to the rest of the country. While in the early nineteenth

---

2.   See Philip McM. Pittman with George M. Covington, *Don't Blame the Treaties: Native American Rights and the Michigan Indian Treaties*, Altwerger and Mandel Publishing Company, Inc., West Bloomfield, Michigan, 1992. The Treaty of Washington of 1836 is printed in its entirely on pp. 178-182.

century the island had a settlement of several dozen people, mostly Native Americans, these residents were gradually moving to the mainland where they were closer to stores and schools. When the descendants of the Williams family sold their island lands to Cleveland Cliffs in 1900 the last remnants of a settlement disappeared. (Even today the island, with an area of 22 square miles, has a permanent population of zero.) No wonder that some Chippewa a hundred years ago thought they could hunt and fish on the island at will. They thought that part of it belonged to them by the Treaty of Washington, and they believed that all of it was available for hunting to them, since it was not settled. But William Mather, from the big city of Cleveland, Ohio, now controlled that island, and he had very different ideas.

Against this background, Jimmy Kishketog was a relict, an old Chippewa Indian born before any white men came to the area, and fully formed as a young hunter before the new white authorities arrived. To him, hunting was not only a necessity but also a claim for freedom—a sense of being in the wild without rules, as his ancestors always had been.

George Genry was also part-Chippewa, but his relationship to the new laws was more complicated since he was also an employee of the U.S. government, the Light House Establishment, and therefore felt the reach of regulations far more than his friend Jimmy Kishketog. But Genry shared Kishketog's contempt for the new game regulations; furthermore, his livelihood was affected by the new laws, since the game animals of Grand Island were essential parts of his family's diet. By hosting Kishketog at North Light and abetting his poaching, Genry was clever. If Kishketog were ever caught, Genry could maintain he knew nothing about the poaching activities. Meanwhile, Kishketog got game for himself, for Genry's family, for trade, and for a primitive form of philanthropy in Munising.

Yes, according to many stories still alive today, Kishketog was, in his own way, a philanthropist among the local Chippewa living in Indiantown and elsewhere near Munising. Kishketog, who died a very old man in 1930, is remembered as a generous person. If he knew that a local tribal family was destitute, he would late at night deposit a saddle of deer on their back porch, waiting for no words of appreciation, and disappear into the woods. No one knew, of course, where the deer came from, but occasionally it must have come from Mather's herd on Grand Island. Maybe it was even one of those exotic animals imported by Mather from Norway or Scotland.

Over the years I have met in the Munising area a number of descendants of Grand Island Chippewa; one of the most informative and helpful has been Dolores LeVeque, who is the great-great-great granddaughter of Powers of the Air, the legendary hero of the island; it was Powers of the Air who in 1820 told Lewis Cass and Henry Schoolcraft the native folktales of the island and who repeated those stories to William Cameron, keeper of North Light. Dolores also told me stories about Jimmy Kishketog. It seems that Kishketog never accepted the rules and mores of white society, continuing to live until his last days as a lone hunter defying all game laws.

Jimmy was fabled among Munising residents for his ability to survive in the woods in any conditions. It was said that he could build a wigwam in thirty minutes. First, he would cut many saplings and strip them of their side branches. Then he would bury one end of each sapling in the ground, bend it over, and insert the other end in the ground a few feet away. Doing this many times, he would construct an upside-down basket, which he then covered with pine boughs. If there was snow, he would cover the boughs with it. Inside, he would build a little fire, vented through a small hole in the ceiling, and could safely spend the night even in the middle of a sub-zero blizzard.

On numerous occasions Jimmy was arrested for game poaching, and was once caught red-handed crossing the channel between the island and the mainland with a deer saddle in his canoe. The town authorities could not fine him, because he had no money, but they placed him in the local jail for several weeks. Upon releasing him, they asked him, as was customary, if he had any small requests that would help him in freedom. His reply was "I need a dollar to buy some ammunition; I gotta go deer hunting."

Kishketog lived in a very small cabin in the woods near Indian Town. When he became aged the authorities eventually decided that he could not take care of himself and placed him in the "old people's home" in Chatham. Kishketog intensely disliked the place and on one occasion was accused of trying to burn down the whole building. He explained that he had gotten cold and, as was his habit in such situations, built a fire to keep warm. The fire was on the floor of his room. Convinced that Jimmy had lost his mind, the administrators of the home sent him to the prison for the criminally insane in Newberry. There Kishketog died at an age that no one, not even he, could verify, but he was rumored to be over a hundred years old.

CHAPTER IX

THE LIGHTHOUSE SAGA: A RORSCHACH TEST FOR THE UP

The Upper Peninsula of Michigan was a particularly striking example of the loosely-connected "island communities" that made up the United States in the nineteenth century.[1] These communities were ruled by local, not national, values, many of them in tension with each other. The federal government had little or no constituency in these isolated communities. The social services it would later provide were absent. The sole exception was the public schools, but they were primarily products of local government, not of federal authorities.

The UP was remote, it was a semi-wilderness, and its sparse adult population was largely foreign-born. Among the minority in the UP which was born locally the largest group was Native Americans, who hardly shared the distant federal government's vision of conquest and expansion. The ethnic groups of the Upper Peninsula possessed different folk cultures and often different religions, which led to richness of saga and song, but provided little in the way of connective societal tissue. Finns, French-Canadians, Native Americans, Poles, Cornishmen and Slovenians had little to say to each other and frequently could not even communicate with each other. They drank heavily and fought frequently. Law enforcement was rare. The natural environment was raped without remorse. The wealthy mine owners and timber barons took what they could get, which under the prevailing conditions of lax regulation was a great deal. In towns like Munising and Calumet the men who owned the workers' houses and the logging camps and mines were almost never personally present, ruling through subordinates who were often petty tyrants.

Freedom of behavior outside the work place was in the nineteenth century permitted, however, to almost all men (not women). Workers and lumberjacks could drink, fish, hunt, and whore almost without restriction.

---

1 Robert H. Wiebe, *The Search for Order, 1877-1920,* Hill and Wang, New York, 1967, p. 14.

The land was so sparsely populated that Native Americans, denied of most of their lands by treaty, could often still use the remaining forests and lakes and rivers for sustenance, as they traditionally had done.

But by 1908 distant and impersonal forces were beginning to restrict this freedom of action. "Modernity" was coming to the UP, along with railroads, electricity, the telephone, and the first automobiles. The first tourists began to appear, people wishing to enjoy the air and water of the Lake Superior region. These outsiders demanded superior services and they often offended the local residents who begrudged their relative wealth, their haughty ways, and their intrusion. Michigan passed its first conservation laws and gradually game wardens appeared who tried to enforce them. A few wealthy businessmen like William Mather, Louis Kaufman, and John Longyear set up private reserves where they enforced their own hunting and fishing privileges while denying those to others. Local sheriffs began to jail rambunctious lumberjacks, renegade hunters and Native American "violators." The residents of the Upper Peninsula were losing their freedoms, defined not politically but by the ability to roam the land as they pleased. The authorities tried to secure order by demarcating property lines, posting "no hunting" signs, and promulgating laws. At the same time they reinforced social inequalities. Resentment grew.

In this situation a dramatic and violent event occurred: the disappearance of the keeper of a remote lighthouse and its assistant keeper. The body of the assistant keeper soon came ashore in a drifting boat under uncertain and mysterious circumstances. What did this event mean? The different disaffected factions in a disunited community seized upon the event and each came up with its own version of what *really* happened.

Contrary to almost all local opinion, the high probability is that the government version of what happened in June 1908 is correct. According to that version both Genry and Morrison met natural deaths as a result of a boat accident while they tried to raise fish nets north of the island. As will be elaborated below, to assume that one of the other versions of the story is accurate (that Genry murdered Morrison and fled; that men from the Cleveland-Cliffs Iron Company murdered both) requires too many supplementary and improbable suppositions. But both the town of Munising and the Genry family, rooted in the Upper Peninsula's singular, skeptical, sometimes violent, colorful history could not accept any establishment view. Both Munising and the Genry family, standing on contrasting sides of ethnic and social divides, drew anti-establishment conclusions, but opposite ones. Munising expressed its dislike of Genry, his contrariness, and his Indianness by suspecting him of a heinous crime. Furthermore, the town's citizens, abetted by sensation-seeking newspapers, enjoyed a lurid story. On the other hand, the Genry family expressed its suspicions of the white establishment, its new game laws, and the arrogance and patrician haughtiness of William Mather by blaming him. Thus, the saga of 1908 serves as a Rorschach Test, an example of how different perceptions rooted in social realities and recent history can affect one's view of the truth. What people thought happened at the lighthouse in June, 1908, tells us much about the Upper Peninsula in the early twentieth century.

To oppose the government version and Commander Smith's report one must believe in some sort of conspiracy or cover-up, either a conspiracy by the Genry family, a conspiracy by the Cleveland Cliffs Iron Company, a conspiracy by local people in Munising—such as the coroner and the undertaker—or a cover-up by Timothy Dee and/or Commander James Smith, USN. Or—some combination of these conspiracies and cover-ups.

If one is to believe that the conspiracy was concocted by the Cleveland Cliffs Iron Company, it is appropriate to ask "at what level"? Are we to believe that William Gwinn Mather, a prominent and wealthy entrepreneur from Cleveland, Ohio, actually told his men to "get Genry but don't tell me how you did it?" Or should we believe that the company men on the island did the deed on their own, understanding that Mather wanted Genry off Grand Island, and then swear each other to silence?

According to the Genry family, Cleveland Cliffs "owned" all the authorities: the newspapers, the coroners, the police, the judges. This blanket accusation seems hyperbolic. Yet the fact that there were two different coroner's reports, neither of them pointing to murder, and that both of them are disputed, is revealing, perhaps not of a hidden conspiracy, but of the limited expertise of local coroners and the depth of feelings of people in Munising, their belief that the authorities were always wrong. To be sure, the stories of the conflict between George Genry and the Cleveland Cliffs Iron Company, on the one hand, and Edward Morrison, on the other, are too frequent and well-grounded to be dismissed. But conflict does not necessarily lead to conspiracy and murder.

The veracity of the Genry family version according to which William Mather and the Cleveland Cliffs Iron Company were responsible for George Genry's death is questionable on several counts. George's son and daughter, Ed Genry and Mary Genry Krueger, claimed (perhaps understandably for children) that George was a peaceable man who never caused trouble or got into fights. Yet many other sources—townspeople, assistant keepers, newspaper reporters in several different papers—assert that he was authoritarian, a brawler, a heavy drinker, and a quarrelsome man. We know from official records that a dozen of his assistant keepers resigned, saying they did not want to work under him. Ed and Mary also said when I asked them about the theory that George had murdered Morrison and fled that they had "never heard" such a story, even though practically all of Munising propagated that theory and many newspapers printed it, and such a version was remembered in Munising for decades. Then, later in the same interview with me, Ed Genry contradicted himself and said that the "murder and flight" story was put out by the Cleveland Cliffs Iron Company to cover its own guilt for the murder of their father. Ed Genry also said that almost a month after the disappearance of George his mother had been approached by the local physician, Dr. Theodore Scholtes, and told that Cleveland Cliffs employees on Grand Island "already have the body but don't want to give it up until you pay money." Yet just a few days later George Genry's body was reported found (and the Genry family agreed that it was found) miles away on the Lake Superior shore near Chapel Beach, showing signs of having been in the water a long time. How can these various stories given out by members of the Genry family be reconciled? It seems that they were striking out in several different directions that were similar only in that they all denied that George Genry was a murderer and fled.

The view that both men were murdered by Cleveland Cliffs employees comes only from the Genry family, and the family clearly would have liked to clear his name of suspicion of murder. If the phrase "innocent until proved guilty" has any meaning, William Gwinn Mather and the Cleveland Cliffs Iron Company are innocent.

But if the Genry family story has major problems, so also does the view of many people in Munising that George Genry murdered Morrison and then fled. A major obstacle to this view is that so many people report that George Genry's body was found near Beaver Beach, brought to town, embalmed, and properly buried in Maple Grove Cemetery, where his tombstone stands today. In order to deny this finding one needs to invent a conspiracy involving the captain and crew of the boat *Lyle D.* which brought the body back to Munising, the coroner, the undertaker, the lighthouse keeper Timothy Dee, cemetery workers, and the Genry family; this would be a very large conspiracy, indeed, and one that surely would have broken down—somebody would have talked—in the years and decades since the event. Would this many people lie, and continue to lie for years, in order to enable George Genry's widow to cash in on the insurance policy on his life? Again, such a supposition seems very unlikely, and, just as is the case with the theory indicting William Mather, so also here objective observers would surely say that George Genry is innocent until proved guilty.

After all these years, what is most striking about this story is how passionate people were about it and how they clung to their theories. I was told by one Munising resident in 1975, sixty-seven years after the event, that Genry "definitely killed Morrison." I was told by another, around 1980, seventy-two years after the event, that she thought George's daughter Johanna had gone to George's funeral in Canada in 1951, when "George actually died."

Munising and the Upper Peninsula were places where the authorities had often deceived and ripped off the local populations. Suspicion and rumor abounded. The whites concluded treaties with the Indians, granting them certain rights (including a reservation on Grand Island and in Munising) that were then violated. The Upper Peninsula itself became a part of Michigan, not Wisconsin, through a swindle that as late as 2003 has been called by a U.S. Congressman "illegal."[2] The iron companies lied to conceal the fact that they had promised substantial financial benefit to the Indian guide who led

2   Don Faber, *The Toledo War: The First Michigan-Ohio Rivalry,* The University of Michigan Press, Ann Arbor, 2008, p. 181.

them to the best ore site. The logging and mining companies desecrated the land and gave their employees little reward. When the workers went on strike their employers used violent means against them. The lumberjacks and miners enlivened their existence with drunken bouts and brawls that the local law enforcement agencies, if there were any, usually ignored. People of the Upper Peninsula loved braggadocio and Munising was famous for the ability of its residents to tell tall tales, often rooted in their diverse ethnic backgrounds and enriched by their imaginations, as the eminent folklorist Richard Dorson observed in scholarly papers unknown to the townspeople. People were suspicious of all authorities. The appearance of a few outsiders, such as William Mather and Alexander Agassiz, and conservation officers, who began telling them how they should live and where and when they could hunt triggered resentment. Whenever they could, the locals found ways around the new regulations.

The locals were accustomed to violence and often promoted it. When two men in a remote lighthouse disappeared, many people automatically assumed that murder was involved. The only question was "who murdered whom?" The answers they gave reflected their own social situations, and constituted "multiple visions" of events. Those who disliked the Genrys and their links to native American culture assumed that Genry was the killer. The Genrys, alienated by the community and then oppressed by outsiders such as William Mather, assumed that he and his company, the Cleveland Cliffs Iron Company, were the instigators of murder. Different grievances found their different appropriate interpretations of events. Imagination shaped by social and ethnic perception became much more important than the truth.

So what happened to the keeper and assistant keeper of Old North Lighthouse in 1908? They died in an accident while trying to raise fish nets north of Grand Island, just as the federal government account at the time reported. But no one in the local town believed this government report then and almost no one there believes it today. From their history and their culture the people in the Upper Peninsula have their reasons for doubting all official reports.

The kitchen of the lighthouse in 1972 before
restoration began. Photo by Loren Graham

Patricia Albjerg Graham at south end of island in 1972 preparing on a trail bike to take to the lighthouse 10 miles away a fireplace screen tied to her back.

Meg Graham and Jeanie Wylie taking in 1973 empty window frames from the lighthouse to town to be filled with glass panes. Photo by Loren Graham

Patricia Albjerg Graham in the living room of the lighthouse after restoration. Photo by Loren Graham

Loren Graham painting the roof of the lighthouse during restoration in 1972. Photo by Patricia Albjerg Graham

EPILOGUE

What kind of a person wants to live in a lighthouse? I now realize that I have lived in the Old North Lighthouse on Grand Island longer than any of the keepers since it was built in 1867—longer than William Cameron, longer than George Genry. So the answer to my question reflects not only on them, but also on me.

People who want to live in a lighthouse are in one way or another odd. Maybe they want to get away from something, as Cameron and Genry wanted to escape the prejudices of white society, or as the two female keepers in Michigan City wanted to live their lives together undisturbed. Or maybe they believe that if they are alone they can be more creative. After all Albert Einstein once said that of all professions the one he would like most to have is that of a lighthouse keeper in a lonely station. Or maybe they are seeking beauty, as the Wyeth family of artists have done in a lighthouse off the coast of Maine. Or maybe they are searching for a refuge from the commercialization and shopping malls that mar much of contemporary America, and, increasingly, the rest of the world. Or perhaps they are hopeless romantics, who see in lighthouses something both evocative and friendly; after all, lighthouses are supposed to help other people, the mariners who wonder where they are and seek landmarks. Lighthouses excite contrasting emotions in different people. Ed Genry, son of George, told me that Old North Light was "a terrible place" and said he never wanted to see it again.

For whatever reason, this lighthouse has worked itself into my bones. I recall the first day I crossed the door of this wild, lonely, enchanting, somewhat ominous, beat-up place, and thought "I want this." Now, after all these years, I am an old man looking out of a rehabilitated building when fresh young faces turn up to gawk, as happens more frequently now than earlier. I have to admit that I resent their arrival, just as George Genry did

145

when William Mather sent carriages with tourists north from his new hotel to see the lighthouse. Still, they have hiked for miles to get here, and they have some sense of exertion and adventure as they arrive.

I belong here, and the story of how I came to belong, and why I belong is a rich one. In the process of domesticating the place I have been suffused by history, not just that of Old North Lighthouse, but of all lighthouses and of the entire Upper Peninsula of Michigan. By learning why and how lighthouses exist, how the appearance of this island fits into the evolution of the Upper Peninsula, why this isolated tower was built, what happened to the keepers who lived in it, and how their lives and deaths fitted into the evolution, natural and social, of the area surrounding it, I have absorbed, and been affected by, the entire history of lighthouses and of this remote part of my country. I do not consider myself an historian of the area and my subject, but a participant in them. As a participant, I am prejudiced, just like all the characters in the story I have told, but in my own way. Objectivity escaped us all, but along different paths. And I celebrate my prejudices, just as many of them did theirs. They were a little strange, and I am a little strange. In my grander moments I would like to think that I have created a different kind of history, an embedded, personal history, somewhere between, and hopefully more revealing, than the impersonal account of the professional historian or the narrow account of the memoirist.

The modern world has a way of draining out the romance of places. When the Chippewa were the only people who lived here, practically every location had its mystical stories. On the high cliffs, in the dark forests, and hovering above the lakes, everywhere there were spirits. There was Wawabezowin and his enormous rope swing on the Painted Rocks; Kaubina and his magic arrow on Grand Island; Mishosha and his charmed canoe on Lake Superior; Waubwenonga, the king of the birds; Manabozho the trickster; Shingwauk and Powers of the Air, who transformed themselves into insects riding on the backs of birds and traveled as fast as the wind.

Today's world has no time or patience, it seems, for such stories. The pioneer store keeper in Munising, W. A. Cox, could not keep accounts with the fanciful names of the local Indians, so he transformed them, not into insects and birds, as Powers of the Air once claimed he could do, but into simple Anglicized surnames. Powers of the Air became "Jim Clark."

Munising is today not the same as it was in 1908. Many of the rough edges have been smoothed. In fact, it is a rather respectable little town, less colorful and interesting than before but more pleasant and just. It has only a handful of bars, one paper mill, a state prison, and in the summers it is a magnet for tourists. Grand Island has become a National Recreation Area under the jurisdiction of the US Forest Service, which has permitted twelve families to continue to be owners and caretakers of aged cottages on the island, as they had been for many previous decades. Munising has graduated from the stage in which it was governed by local values to being another town in a large nation submitting to local, state, and national rules.

Yet the person who knows Munising's past and looks for remnants of it will find them. Munising is even yet not mainstream America but a somewhat idiosyncratic community. Where else would you have an "outhouse race" (in nearby Trenary) or a dog sled race finishing in the main downtown intersection, which got its first stop light last year? A recent mayor of Munising, Rod DesJardins, is a descendant of one of the oldest French fur-trading families, and in his rough camaraderie one can detect rooted family characteristics. People in the UP are still proud of their distinct qualities and boast about the infamous "Yoopers" as unique individuals. I have met people in Munising who have never in their lives been in a large city.

An illustration of how Munising today has changed from what it was in 1908 yet retains some of its earlier characteristics is provided by my very recent experience there. A number of people in the town who know that I have been working on this book on the lighthouse saga have on several occasions asked me to talk about it. These events have been held in a local bookstore-restaurant (The Falling Rock), in the home of an island family, at an arts and crafts festival near the city dock in the center of the town, at the Alger County Historical Society, and at a "Life on Lake Superior" celebration on the island.

When I have told the story and presented three alternative explanations for it (Genry killed Morrison and fled; both were accidentally killed [the government version]; William Mather ordered the deaths) most people are now unfamiliar with the event. So much time has passed, three generations, that many local people have forgotten the story. Nobody has a personal memory of George Genry anymore and therefore nobody has a reason to dislike him as an individual. However, usually there is somebody in the group who says something like "yes, I remember that my grandmother told me about this, but I don't recall the details." Yet despite the disappearance of a town memory of the event, when today's local residents hear the story from me they usually rather quickly come to an opinion about what "actually" happened. As was the case long ago, the government version is the least popular. But instead of throwing the blame on Genry, as the people tended to do a century ago, now they favor the view "Mather did it." This shifts reveals, I think, both change and continuity in the Munising community.

Behind the old interpretation that Genry murdered Morrison and fled was prejudice against Indians, especially aggressive ones like Genry. People in Munising have now learned that the expression of such rank prejudice is no longer acceptable. It is almost inconceivable that anyone today would defend his position in the way in which Morrison's brother did in 1908 when he wrote the government accusing Genry of the crime and then signed his letter "A White American." To be sure, irritation against Native Americans still exists in the area, especially when the natives benefit from special fishing rights, such as use of gill nets banned for other fishermen. But the arguments against the Native Americans are no longer made in open ethnic prejudicial terms; instead, the criticism is based on a concept of "fairness," that Indian fishermen should not have rights that others do not. That question is still alive and sensitive in the Munising area.

But one issue on which the Munising of 1908 and the Munising of 2013 are in agreement is what might be called "anti-establishment" views. Munising still thinks the authorities, especially the federal government, frequently get things wrong, do not understand local issues, and cannot be trusted. Sometimes this view takes a sharply right-wing or libertarian cast. At other times it is just based on local rootedness or pride. Whatever the motivation, Munising still today does not like the federal government's explanation that both Genry and Morrison died accidentally. The story has to be more complicated and conspiratorial than that. And since it is no longer acceptable to throw the blame on the Indians, the preference – when evoked by my story-telling – is to blame the distant big company people, in other words, Mather and Cleveland-Cliffs.

Munising is still, over a century after these events, nursing grievances against distant powerful authorities. The largest employers in the town, the paper mill and the prison, remain non-local. The process of the homogenization of the previously-distinct local communities of America into a single national fabric that the historian Robert Wiebe described as happening in the twentieth century is still, in Munising's case, not complete.

When I first came to the isolated lighthouse some of the romance of the place still resided here, heightened by the fact that it was a ruin, and one with an ominous history. While I enjoyed the emotions, even the uneasy ones, that ran through me when I explored the place and learned something of its history, I realize now that inadvertently I have been destroying what I enjoyed. Tourists who hike to the lighthouse now see a restored building, pristine and less interesting. And this erosion of romance will only increase. After my wife and I are no longer able to care for the place, which will be in a few years, we intend to give it away so that it can be a museum open to the public. Already a bus for tourists exists on the southern part of the island and after the museum is created it will bring them to the lighthouse itself. No longer will people wishing to see it have to hike ten miles.

Although the romance of the place is less now than it used to be, at night or when fog envelopes the place, I still feel the foreboding thrill that I first experienced in the place more than fifty years ago. When will that feeling disappear entirely? Probably when the first tourist bus pulls up at the back door. But then perhaps not, if those same tourists who are driven to our back door can then be lured back to experiencing a world we have lost.

ACKNOWLEDGMENTS

irst of all, I would like to thank the good people of Munising, where my wife and I, taken together, have spent our summers for over 75 years. There is a special pleasure, known to few in contemporary America, in walking down a street and meeting several people on every block whom you know and exchanging cheery greetings with them. These people have helped me over the decades to collect the material for this story. It is impossible for me to name all of them but I would like to name at least a few. Dolores LeVeque, Native American descendant of the original people of Grand Island, has been a constant help, almost an official assistant, in recording a history in which earlier versions often omitted the role of the local Chippewa (Ojibway, Anishinaabeg). The Chippewa culture was almost extinguished in the area but is now coming back rather strongly. Julia Cameron, another helper, was one of the last in the area to speak the native language fluently, but now more speakers are appearing, aided by language teaching promoted by the tribe.

Other residents of Munising who played important roles include two past presidents of the Alger County Historical Society, Isabella Sullivan and Mary Jo Cook. In addition, I remember the important assistance given me by John Lezotte (past caretaker of Grand Island for the Cleveland-Cliffs Iron Company), his brother Tony Lezotte (former mayor and tug-boat captain, who illuminated me on the old Munising lumberjack culture), Harry Powell (descendant of one of the first white families in the area and last permanent resident on the island), Peter Benzing (an idiosyncratic assistant on all projects), John Carr (an indefatigable explorer of the island who helps many people, including me), Jeff and Nancy Dwyer (proprietors of the Falling Rock Café, a unique center of history, music, and local culture), K Witty and Brett Nikkari (friends who do not fear difficult tasks), Lewis DesJardins and his son Rod (descendants of fur traders in the region; Rod also served as mayor of the town), William Cox (one of the last residents of the town who remembered George Genry), Charlie and Barbara Stark (enthusiasts for the island and its history), the Van Landschoot family (commercial fishermen who have helped me get off and on the island in bad weather). And then there are the descendants of George Genry who granted me interviews: Johanna Genry, Ed Genry, and Mary Genry Krueger. Jo Lee Dibert-Fitko, great-niece of Edward Morrison, gave me valuable photographs.

Bernie Bugg, a resident of Munising, helped me in a special way. He is the root of the only statements in the book that I know are not actually true: the story in the introduction of how I found the newspaper clippings in the lighthouse kitchen on the disappearance of Genry and Morrison is actually a description of how Bernie found them at the time that I was beginning the restoration. He generously gave the clippings to me. This is the only place in the book where I took literary license.

Among the summer people on the island individuals who stand out as helpers are Kathie and Phil Carlson. Kathie read over an early version of the book and propelled me to improve it. Fellow Trout Bayers – the Barnett, Jossi, and Erickson extended families – have all heard from me versions of this story and have encouraged me further.

In the nearby city of Marquette Kaye Hiebel, executive director of the Marquette Regional History Center, is a tireless promoter of local history and the preservation of Old North Lighthouse. In the same center, Rosemary Michelin, librarian of the John M. Longyear Research Library, not only helped me with the local archives but read and critiqued an early version of the manuscript. Jack Deo, who has compiled a remarkable collection of historical photographs in his Superior View Studio, supplied many of the photographs in the book. Russell Magnaghi, professor of history at Northern Michigan University, deserves much credit for assembling an extensive list of sources on Upper Peninsula history. Not far from Marquette, Alice Paquette of the Houghton County Museum, helped me find sources. Keith Payne, Interpretive Ranger, Keweenaw National Historical Park, took photographs of the statue of Alexander Agassiz and assisted me in exploring the history of the Calumet and Hecla Mining Company.

Farther afield, at the Western Reserve Historical Society in Cleveland, Ohio, Ann Sindelar, Reference Supervisor, and Vicki Catozza, Library Assistant, explored together with me the papers and diaries of

William Gwinn Mather, longtime president of the Cleveland Cliffs Iron Company.

Richard Dorson, a founder of folklore studies in the United States, and a professor of history at Indiana University, ignited my interest in the folklore of the Upper Peninsula when I joined his department as a young professor. At the time I had no idea how importantly what he was telling me would fit into the story in this book.

The Library of Congress in Washington DC contains an invaluable collection on American folklore. It was there that I listened to the songs collected in and near Munising by Alan Lomax in the nineteen thirties. Todd Harvey and Judith Gray of the American Folklore Center there showed me how to listen to those songs of long ago.

Last, there are family members and close friends who for decades have indulged and assisted me as I worked on this book. First of all, my wife, Patricia Albjerg Graham, whose grandfather was a Baptist minister to the local Grand Island Native Americans in the nineteenth century, who knew the keepers of Old North Light, and who left a massive collection of diaries and letters, all today in the lighthouse. Pat is not only my very closest friend, for life, but also an inspiration to me at moments when "things get too hard." Our daughter Meg is cut from the same cloth. In addition, she did heroic work in the restoration of the lighthouse at a time when the task seemed hopeless. Having such a family made the rewarding life that we have had not only possible but a deep pleasure.

Among the several close friends who have encouraged me along the way are Sheila Biddle, who has starred in this role for decades, Donald Fanger, and Elisabeth Hansot and David Tyack, all of whom read the manuscript and made encouraging suggestions.

In closing, let me celebrate the lighthouse and its island. A deep reward in any life is feeling an intimate connection to a place, a geographical spot. I have had the good fortune of having that experience.

Loren Graham
Old North Lighthouse, Grand Island
May, 2013

Index

Tyack, David, 153
U. S. Army, 95, 106
U. S. Coast Guard, 8, 83, 115, 116
U. S. Forest Service, 147
U. S. Lighthouse Board, 95
U. S. Lighthouse Establishment, 94, 95, 106, 109, 131
U. S. Lighthouse Service, 15, 90, 116
U. S. Navy, 95, 106, 107
University Hospitals, Cleveland, 74
University of Virginia, 74
Upper Peninsula
    early history, 21 ff.
    copper and iron industries, 34, 44, 69
    folklore, 53, 135
    labor strife, 36-41
    logging, 59
    and William Mather, 74
    transformation by modernity, 136-137
    skepticism toward authority, 140

Van Dein, Ed, 54, 127
Van Dusen, William, 15, 17
Van Landschoot family, 53, 152
Victoria Hotel, Munising, 58
Walker family, 63
Washington, George, 83, 85
Washington Post, 101
Washington School, 63
Waubewonga, 93, 146
Wawabezowin, 93, 146
Welsh, 53
Western Federation of Miners, 37, 40
Western Reserve Historical Society, 31, 72, 152
Western Reserve University (Case Western Reserve University), 74
Wetmore, 45, 51
White, Peter, 67, 68
Whitefish Point, 33
Wiebe, Robert H., 11, 105, 135, 149
Wigman, Richard, 15, 17
Williams family, 89, 130